"*Define Your Own Way* is a common sense guide providing the essential tools for young African American females to grow into successful and well-rounded African American women. Being an African American woman raised in the inner city by a single mother, I understand the importance of being well-rounded and self-motivated. Working in the community, it has become challenging and heartbreaking to watch the self-worth and self-esteem of young women plummet. This low self-esteem can cause them to make poor choices that can affect their lives in a major way. *Define Your Own Way* is an essential resource to help young women get on track to becoming the well-formed, self-motivated women of their dreams."

—**Towalame Austin, President of the Magic Johnson Foundation, Inc.**

"Nicole Roberts Jones has outlined the pathway for aspiring black women in *Define Your Own Way*. As her church pastor in her pivotal years, I witnessed firsthand her structured movement of at-risk girls from zero to hero, modeling the design for the program now subsumed under Imani Phi Christ, which was born as a sorority for sorrowing sisters, pulling the queen to her rightful status in human dignity, using the magnet of personal desire as the power source of the divine. Getting inside the spirit, the founding mother turns on a light that illuminates the way home—home to your knowledge of the history of those upon whose shoulders you stand, home to your progression to the next stage of destined development, home to the joy that comes with knowing who you are and whose you are. And the best is yet to come!"

—**Rev. Cecil L. "Chip" Murray, Pastor (retired),**
First African Methodist Episcopal (FAME) Church, Los Angeles
Tansey Chair, Center for Religion, University of Southern California

"Many young African American women are without the relevant and real resources that are needed and required to mature God's way. Nicole Roberts Jones has provided it in *Define Your Own Way*, by creating a vital map for navigating the often treacherous road toward womanhood. She is hip, historical, and helpful with a sprinkling of hallelujahs!"

—**Rev. Dr. Sheron C. Patterson, author of**
Put On Your Crown: The Black Woman's Guide to Living Single (and Christian)
and an ordained United Methodist Church minister

Define Your Own Way

Define Your Own Way

Empowering
Young
African
American
Women

NICOLE ROBERTS JONES

THE PILGRIM PRESS

CLEVELAND

This book is dedicated to African American woman everywhere—
from the inner city to suburbia,

in boardrooms,

outer offices,

home offices, and

classrooms.

It is for ALL of us who find ourselves at the crossroads
of possibility, promise, perspective, passion, and purpose.
The pages of this book contain my earnest prayer that each of you will
define your own way and live the life of your dreams!

The Pilgrim Press, 700 Prospect Avenue, Cleveland, Ohio 44115
thepilgrimpress.com
© 2010 by Nicole Roberts Jones

Scripture quotations not otherwise noted are from the New Revised Standard
Version of the Bible, © 1989 by the Division of Christian Education of the
National Council of Churches of Christ in the United States of America,
and are used by permission. Changes have been made for inclusivity.

SUSTAINABLE Certified Fiber
FORESTRY Sourcing
INITIATIVE
Label applies to the text stock www.sfiprogram.org

Printed in the United States of America on acid-free paper
14   13   12   11   10   5   4   3   2   1
Library of Congress Cataloging-in-Publication Data
Jones, Nicole Roberts, 1969–
      Define your own way : empowering young African American women /
Nicole Roberts Jones.
          p. cm.
      ISBN 978-0-8298-1870-3
      1. African American women—Conduct of life.   2. African American
women—Religious life.   3. Success—Religious aspects—Christianity.   I. Title.
BJ1610.J66 2010
248.8'4308996073—dc22   2010022020

CONTENTS

⊠

FOREWORD

With extraordinary insight and sensitivity, Nicole Roberts Jones, a trained social worker and life coach, offers a wealth of information and guidance for African American women between the ages of eighteen and thirty. Nicole is founder and CEO of Imani Corporation, a unique organization that grew out of her work with teens through a program called Imani Phi Christ she began after observing the destructive behavior of some young people in the wake of the Los Angeles riots of 1992. Nicole, though only two years out of college, realized that she could use her own life experiences as well as communication skills she had acquired in the entertainment industry to mentor and coach young women who sorely needed guidance and support to improve their lives. Determined to acquire appropriate education and skills necessary to fulfill her task, Nicole pursued a master's degree in social work, which she quickly put to use organizing more Imani Phi

Christ chapters and teaching mentoring techniques to women in cities across the country.

While most of Nicole's work experience has been with adolescent and young adult African American woman, the principles she teaches can be easily adapted for women of all ages and all races. Through a weekly blog, Internet radio show, and now this book, Nicole models her universal message of living out one's life to the fullest. *Define Your Own Way* contains eight chapters, each of which addresses specific issues facing young African American women. Topics include goal setting in a society that often encourages short-term gratification, developing a positive self-image and self-esteem in an environment where negative images prevail, and building positive relationships. Nicole shares aspects through the lens of her own deeply held Christian faith.

Nicole successfully combines experience and clinical observation to offer practical and relevant solutions to challenges commonly faced by young women today. She honestly and perceptively provides simple tools for self-examination that can lead young women to make solid life choices. This book will serve as a guide to a better life for a generation. I highly recommend *Define Your Own Way* as a tool for gaining inner confidence and achieving material success.

Adrienne Lash Jones, PhD
Professor Emeritus
African American Studies &
Women's Studies, Oberlin College

ACKNOWLEDGMENTS

I must acknowledge all the folks who have helped me define my own way as an author and made writing this book possible.

First, I thank Dr. Cecil L. "Chip" Murray, retired pastor of First AME Church in Los Angeles, California, the man who planted the spiritual seed that became my purpose. His belief in the idea of Imani Phi Christ gave birth to my life's purpose in 1993. His nurturing and support strengthened Imani's foundation and allowed it to take flight.

I also thank a group of mentors, none of whom I have met, but who have each watered seeds in my spirit, which have helped me grow. This group of preachers, authors, teachers, and visionaries helped shape my life and my message, and helped me define my own way. These "silent" mentors include: Oprah Winfrey, Marian Wright Edelman, Maya Angelou, Ella Baker, Mary

McLeod Bethune, Joyce Meyer, T. D. Jakes, Charles Swindoll, and Bishop Noel Jones, to name a few. You each have left me a rich legacy on which to draw. Because you each defined your own way, I am able to light the path for others to come behind me.

I must also thank a group of my girlfriends and family who encouraged me to write a book and/or prayed for me during the writing process. Thank you's go to Mommy, Daddy, Auntie Faye, Cousin Tracy, Teri Lynn, Carmonique, Mechellet, Montrese, Erika, Amelia and Milca, Linda, Gina, Chenita, and my AKA sisters of Psi Omega Chapter. A very special thank you goes to the members of the Imani Corporation board of directors, who are truly "the wind beneath my wings." I especially want to acknowledge Mrs. Jeanette Conrad Ellis, who, by sharing her own writing experience, inspired me to become an author. Your sisterhood in authorship and life is truly a blessing. I must also recognize a group of folks who were brave enough to read the first draft of this book and share their valuable insights: Mercedes Nelson, BeNeca Ward, and Dr. Adrienne Lash Jones. Mercedes (my line sister!!) and BeNeca, thank you for being the kind of girlfriends willing to give of your busy schedules to read the first draft of this book and for sharing your valuable insight. Adrienne, my mentor mother-in-law, then took it from there as she changed my typos into grammatical art and shared with me her insight from years of teaching. My writing and insight has increased because of time spent with her in writing this book.

I had to save the best acknowledgements for last. First, I am so grateful to my husband, Dr. Darryl Jones, the man who gives a voice to all of my dreams. His initial push made me sit with pen to paper to begin writing this book. He often thinks I do not listen to his strong urgings, yet this book is evidence that I do listen to my coach! So keep yelling out those plays, baby! Every player definitely needs a coach to push her into possibility. What a blessing to have found that in you! "Thank you" would never be enough to tell you what your love, partnership, and support mean to me.

Above all else, the ultimate thank you goes to God! I give YOU the highest praise, for through you, I found *my own way.* Thank you, God, for shining your light on my path, which allowed me to find my life's purpose. Your light led me to establish Imani and, ultimately, write this book. You poured into me vision and inspiration. I pray that every woman who reads these pages will find the same gift of divine purpose that through my deepening relationship with you, I too, have found.

INTRODUCTION
My Defining Journey

For as long as I can remember, I wanted to work in the entertainment industry. And, only two years after graduating from college, I found myself doing just that. There I was in 1993 working on the hottest TV show, being invited to all the hip Hollywood parties, where I bumped elbows with all the biggest stars. Hollywood became my life. My lifelong dream had been realized. Yet after investing eight years in the entertainment business and making great headway in fulfilling what I thought would be my life's vocation, I found myself thinking back to my ancestors. I thought about those who fought so that I could live my dream. I thought of people like Rosa Parks, Martin Luther King Jr., Mary McLeod Bethune, Fannie Lou Hamer, Ella Baker, Coretta Scott King, Josephine Baker, Dr. Maya Angelou, and Marian Wright Edelman. As these torches lit the fire in my mind, I began to ask myself, "How do I want to be remembered? Whose life am I touching?" I determined then that I wanted my life to have more than a superficial impact. As I progressed professionally in an industry that allows its consumers to escape reality, I realized that I was ignoring a painful reality that existed right under my nose: African American teenagers who were losing hope. As I drove in and out of the inner city each day to conquer Hollywood, the images I saw in my own neighborhood became much more powerful than any entertainment gig or party. The plight I saw while living in riot-torn South Central Los Angeles was tugging at my soul.

As I thought about how blessed I was to be able to live out my dreams, I couldn't help ponder why I had made it when many others from my neighborhood hadn't. Growing up in a socioeconomically disadvantaged community had not hindered my personal progress. So why had it for so many others? The more I thought about it, the more fired up I became. While I knew that I could not change the fact that some of my friends from the neighborhood had not made it, I knew that I could help to keep that from being a reality for those who came behind me. I would use the torch that I have been given to blaze new trails for another generation.

As I continued to ponder what I could do to renew the hope of a new generation, I was given the opportunity to volunteer at a youth lock in at my church. I found myself in a room filled with three hundred youth, all of whom seemed to be struggling and losing hope. I immediately connected with them because I had been exactly where they were just ten years earlier. Before I knew it, I had marched up to the minister of youth and asked why there were no programs for teenage girls. He responded, "Why don't *you* start one?" Me? Start a program? I could feel my heart jump into my throat. How would I accomplish such a huge task? Why hadn't I just kept quiet!? I only volunteered to be a foot soldier, not the general of an army. I wondered what I had gotten myself into. As I questioned the decision to undertake the task and even to suggest it, I remembered all of the things that made it possible for me to be successful, for me to "make it." You see, I had made it from high school to college without becoming another statistic of early pregnancy and gun violence. And, I had made it to a place where I could define for myself who I wanted to be. But what made the difference for me?

My mind flooded with memories of those who had sown the seeds in my life that allowed me to make it. I remembered how I had watched my YMCA summer camp counselor, Cheryl, whom I met when I was twelve, prepare for law school by studying for the LSAT. Watching her helped me dream of the possibility of higher education. I also remembered the not-so-pleasant events that shaped my young life, such as the time when only fifteen minutes after my mom made me leave the skating rink there was a shooting that left many people injured, some dead. My mind flashed back to phone calls I received in college about the growing number of drive-by shootings in the neighborhood or to the number of friends who had babies in high school, and those who had gone to jail for selling drugs.

Then my thoughts turned to the things that kept me grounded. For example, I participated in community service projects while in high school. My friends and I had lots of fun washing cars to raise money for field trips or visiting residents in convalescent homes. These memories reignited my passion to give back. I also remembered how my mother made me go to church every Sunday, despite my resistance. Her small nudge instilled in me the importance of faith and also planted within me a belief in a higher power and purpose.

Three ideals emerged from these memories: faith, sisterhood, and service. These ideals became the basis for a new organization for teenage girls. And, on September 19, 1993, I committed myself to answering the urgent call to create an organization that would change the lives of young women. This urgent call lit a spark inside me I had never felt before. Once the idea entered my spirit, I immediately moved forward with it. In fact, I stayed up all night developing the concept of this new sisterhood. I even got as detailed as developing bylaws and ceremonies. I needed a name that would embody my vision for empowering women to become all they could be. For me, the keys to my becoming all that I could be were faith in Christ and faith in myself. So, I used a Swahili dictionary to find appropriate words to help young African American women take pride in our faith and African heritage. I found that the word for faith in Swahili is *Imani*. I next decided on the Greek letter *phi* to give the organization a traditional sorority feel, a sisterly and positive place for girls to belong. And, of course, Christ represented the faith in which the organization would be grounded. That night, Imani Phi Christ was born.

As I worked tirelessly through the night, a fire in my belly was fueled in ways the entertainment industry never could. I had found my life's purpose. At that moment, I began to define my own way.

What began as one chapter at the First AME Church of Los Angeles grew to ten chapters nationwide. The primary goal of Imani Phi Christ, then and now, is to maximize the potential of African American teenage girls everywhere. Since its inception, over three hundred girls have joined. The program offers personal development, mentorship, college preparation, and financial literacy programs. Ninety-nine percent of our young women graduate high school; 95 percent become college graduates. What was conceived in one night has emerged into more than seventeen years of defining moments for many young women.

ANOTHER DEFINING MOMENT

Some fourteen years after Imani Phi Christ was formed, I was moved to respond on a broader scale to the urgent cry from some African American young women. First, many of the girls with whom I had worked over the years had become young women. They were high school and college graduates who were trying to define themselves as young women. Because they continued to call me for advice and guidance, and began to refer their friends to do the same, it became clear to me that there was a void in information and support available to this group of women ages eighteen to thirty. It is because of this need that I also founded a program for African American adult women, Imani Life Transformations, which is partially responsible for this book emerging.

I was also motivated to write this book by some not-so-pleasant words. You may remember them: nappy-headed ho'es. These words spoken by talk radio personality Don Imus to describe the championship Rutgers University women's basketball team was like a shot that rang all over America. Three words, blurted out by a Caucasian man who obviously had no respect for African American women, created another defining moment in my life. My initial reaction was obviously anger at Don Imus. Then I thought about how I had heard African American women call each that same thing or worse. Sure, we can say it's not what people call you, it's what you answer to, but so many of our young black women have been called out of their names for so long, they have begun to answer to these derogatory names. To make matters worse, some of us had even begun to dress and talk in ways that reflect this name-calling and create a less than positive image. I began to question what was happening to us. How did we come to this?

I believe the civil rights fight of the 1960s has come full circle, as we have found ourselves right back in the fight for hope and opportunity. Yet, this time we are not fighting to have hope and opportunity but to partake in it. We are fighting for dignity and respect. However, this time the fight is to receive dignity and respect for ourselves as well as from our own people. This new fight calls for each of us to look in the mirror. It calls us to reclaim what we stand for as a people. If we are to find what we have lost, we must uproot the seeds that were planted that got us to this place. It is time for us as a people to chart our own course and DEFINE our *own* way!

I am not pointing my finger at anyone. As a young girl from the inner city, I wanted to be "down" with my 'hood, too. So I am ashamed to admit that I was guilty of using derogatory language to describe myself and other women. Although my parents had taught me what it was to be a woman; I still chose to accept the less than positive images that surrounded me. But one day it hit me that I had all but rejected the "black and proud" image my parents instilled in me from the '60s civil rights movement and the "hold your head up high" sentiment passed down through my elders. That was my light bulb moment. One day I heard my ancestors call, and I knew I needed to reclaim what I had lost and that I needed to help others find their way as well.

Now my message has expanded not only to teenage girls but to a broader audience of young women. Many of these women seem to have become lost in the crowd that wanted to be "down," and were willing to sacrifice their dignity and respect to do it. This book emerges out of my desire to help young women expel the negative images placed on them by the media, or even by themselves, and to encourage them to define themselves in ways that honor themselves and those who came before them. It is my sincere prayer that the pages of this book will help young women find their way by defining their way, and that our ancestors will look down with pride and confidence that their legacy was not in vain.

Woman, if the soul of the nation is to be saved, I believe that you must become its soul.

—Coretta Scott King

1

WHAT WOULD THEY SAY?

The eyes of the future are looking back
at us and they are praying for us to see
beyond our own time.

—Terry Tempest Williams

If our ancestors could come forward in time what would they say to us?

Whenever I ask myself this powerful question, I am forced to think introspectively about where we have been and where we are going. I think of all that our ancestors went through so that we can make all of our dreams come true. I think of how our ancestors came to America as slaves stacked on top of one another on slave ships, enduring the stench of each others' urine, feces, and menstrual flow. I think of how many died on the journey and how those who survived faced a very different life in America. I think of how our ancestors stood on auction blocks, picked cotton day in and day out in the hot sun, and how they went without shoes and proper clothing and had to make meals from scraps they received from Massa's kitchen. I think of the fact that most slaves were not allowed to learn to read or to write. I think of the fact that even after slavery ended our African American foreparents were not allowed to live in certain neighborhoods, to buy the home of their choice, eat at certain restaurants, go to certain schools, or exercise the right to vote. I realize how necessary it was for our ancestors to fight hard for freedom. More than anything, contemplating the struggles of our ancestors makes me wonder if I am making our ancestors proud. Am I fulfilling the goals and dreams their sacrifices allow me to achieve?

We stand on some very broad shoulders. We are here today because of the price paid by many of our ancestors, including great writers like Ida B. Wells, Gwendolyn Brooks, and Zora Neale Hurston; entertainers like Josephine Baker, Leontyne Price and Katherine Dunham; and activists like Sojourner Truth and Harriet Tubman. Some our ancestors, like Mary McLeod Bethune, Shirley Chisholm, and Barbara Jordan, broke down the walls in government, while others played the game well, like athletes Wilma Rudolph and Althea Gibson, or invented hair care products, like Madame C. J. Walker. Others worked in math and science, wrote poems, gave speeches, listened to others' problems, and broke down countless racial and gender barriers. These women, as well as many other sung and unsung heroines, paved our way.

In light of their struggles, I sometimes wonder what our ancestors would have to say about us today. In some ways, I think they would beam with pride over the accomplishments of women like media mogul Oprah Winfrey. And surely they would cry and clap their hands to see that a descendant of slaves, Michelle Obama, now stands as the First Lady of the United States of America.

Their pride and excitement might be dampened, however, by negative images of African Americans that continue to dominate the media and pierce the minds and hearts of many today. They would be outraged at Don Imus, yes; but they would be equally outraged at those who call us the same names Imus called us.

If our ancestors could come forward in time
what would they say to us?

When I ponder this question, I am forced to look deeply inside myself for the answer. I am reminded of all that our ancestors went through so that you and I can be and do *anything* we dream of. And I wonder if we are living up to their expectations or whether they would think that what they did for us was in vain? Our ancestors not only maximized their potential for themselves but also for the benefit of others who would come behind them. They had to fight hard to obtain the American dream. We owe our very own existence to their legacy. I wonder how our ancestors would feel about who we have become, individually and collectively. I sometimes wonder if we are squandering the legacy we've inherited in ways that will negatively impact those who come behind us.

That is why Terry Tempest Williams's quote at the beginning of this chapter is so powerful. The eyes of the future are, indeed, looking at us and praying that we see beyond our own time, which requires us to live for tomorrow, instead of just living for today. The legacy that every young woman leaves depends on what she does today. Every young adult woman must ask herself what kind of example she is leaving for others to follow. Is it a shining example or one that is tarnished? Is her light shining in ways that future children and grandchildren can follow and reap the benefits? Is her life paying homage to our ancestors?

When I think about how our ancestors see us I then begin to think about how I want to be remembered. I think of those who came before me. I think of all the opportunities I have had because someone else paved the way. I think of the fact that I am a black woman with a master's degree from Inglewood, California, whose life could have been defined very differently based on where I grew up. I don't take for granted the opportunity that I was able to obtain an education, especially since so many who came before me could not. I do not take for granted that I learned to read and write without having to face the beatings many of my enslaved foreparents suffered when trying to become educated. I do not take for granted that I have been able to pursue a career because of those who blazed trails before me. Above all else, I do not take for granted that I rose above the odds.

These thoughts have put a fire in my belly to help African American young adult women define their own way, to reach out and grab the fruit of our ancestors' labors by realizing and living in their *maximum* potential. Yes, it is time for the spirit of who you are to spring forth from the inside out. It is time for you to work on defining yourself, so that we can truly become the collective village full of the gorgeous, powerful, articulate, spiritual, and intelligent women we *really* are!

How do we do this? What does it mean to define your own way? In a nutshell, a woman who has defined who she is has worked to become fulfilled, healthy, happy, and complete. She performs in her area of passion and purpose in everything she does as a daughter, mother, wife, worker, student, volunteer, community leader, and anything else she touches. But how does a woman get to that end result?

Throughout the course of this book, I will use each of the letters in the word *define* to help you define your own way. First allow me to introduce the meaning of each letter in the word **DEFINE** as the remaining chapters will describe each in more detail.

DISCOVERY

First, the *D* in *DEFINE* stands for discovery. Before we can define our own way, we must unearth anything that may be keeping us from reaching our maximum potential. We must also be willing to do whatever it takes to move out of our way any barriers to self-definition. Once we discover and remove any roadblocks, we are then free to discover our purpose, and passion.

EDIFICATION

Second, the *E* in *DEFINE* stands for edification. We must be committed to the lifelong process of edification or building ourselves up, both inside and out, physically, financially, mentally, and spiritually. We must constantly embrace opportunities to learn, grow, and improve ourselves.

FAITH

Next, as you may have been able to guess, *F* is for faith. We must have faith, which scripture defines as "the substance of things hoped for, the evidence of things not seen." (Heb. 11:1 NKJ) We must believe in ourselves and in the God, who uniquely made each of us.

INVESTMENT

The *I* in *DEFINE* stands for investment. We must take care to invest our time and energy in activities and people who are capable of yielding a positive return. On the flip side, we must avoid activities and people who drain our time and other resources without our receiving any sort of return for our investment.

Nurture

N stands for nurture. Once we discover where we can best invest our energies, we must nurture the relationships and activities that will reap the greatest return on our investment. All people need to nurture and be nurtured. We must avoid or be willing to let go of relationships and activities that do not nurture the seed of hope and opportunity within us.

Essence

Lastly, *E* stands for essence. Our essence is the core of our being. It springs from our soul, spirit, and heart. Even as we grow, we should not allow the essence of who God made us to be to change. For it our essence that allows our lights to shine!

This book calls you to join me on a journey to define your own life. As you embark on this journey, you will uncover and discover various parts of yourself never before explored or that you may have needed to re-explore. If you make the most of this journey, it will help you to begin to live in your maximum zone. Every step in this journey requires you to look deeply into your soul, spirit, and heart. This telescopic look at your inner and outer life will help you build better relationships, more constructively use your gifts, solidify your life's purpose, and ultimately lead to a life you have defined! To further aid you on this journey, you will find "Defining Questions" at the end of each chapter. These questions will help you reflect upon and further explore the topics covered along the way. So fasten your seat belt and get ready to join me on a journey that will define the rest of your life!

The D of Define

DISCOVERY

2

TAKE OFF THAT CAP

Opportunities to pursue fulfillment
would be limited only by the outer margins
of one's individual ability.

—Sidney Poitier, from *Measure of a Man*

The D of DEFINE stands for discovery. Before you set out on the journey to define your own way, you must first discover anything that may be hindering your ability to define and reach your goals. In this chapter, you will uncover some of those hindrances and begin to work on removing them. You will also begin to discover and define a vision for the rest of your life.

Think of your life as a soda bottle with a cap or lid on top of it. The cap is what keeps the drink inside the bottle. If the cap is not removed, the drink stays in the bottle and never gets sipped, nor can the bottle be filled up with more. Seems obvious when put in those terms, right? If we consider this in regards to our own lives, think about what caps you may have placed on your life that may be hindering your progress, keeping your life in the bottle—keeping you right where you are, never to do or be more.

Have you ever asked yourself what limits you may be putting on yourself? Have you ever explored what caps you might be placing on your life? Your caps may have been caused by things that were not in your control, such as having an absent father, growing up without money, not having a supportive family or a family at all, being raped, abused, or hurt, or never feeling good enough.

In his book *Measure of a Man*, actor Sidney Poitier states, "You are not responsible for what has happened but for what you make of it. It is up to each of us to take our own measure, to claim what's real and to answer for yourself." You see, you may not have the power to change what has happened to you in the past or what others may have done to you in the past, but you do have power over how you allow it to affect your present and your future. These experiences can put a cap on you and limit your possibilities, but only if you allow them. So if your dad left, prove to the world you can make it without him! If you were raped or abused, you can take that negative circumstance in your life and figure out how to turn it into positive. By no means am I downplaying the act of abuse or any other thing that may have happened in your life that has made you feel like you can't become who you desire to be. While you cannot change what has happened, you can start from where you are. You can get professional counseling or find a support group to obtain the tools you need to help you move forward with your life. Yes, I know that historically in the African American community seeking mental health counseling has carried a stigma. But seeking counseling does not mean that you are "crazy"; it means you want to get over whatever is hindering your progress. Once you discover and remove what's capping your life, the sky's the limit for you.

Maybe you are struggling with an area in your life because someone in your family made poor choices that have affected you. I have heard some preachers refer to this as a generational curse: "My father was abusive, so now I date abusive men." "My parents went through a bitter divorce, and now I am afraid of relationships." "My mom did drugs, and now I do drugs." "I never knew my father, and now I believe all men are trifling." "My mother had a very bad attitude, so now I have one too." "I was raped, and now I have a bad sexual outlook."

It is important that you stop and recognize those things that may have happened so that you do not passively allow negative patterns to develop in your life. Whatever it may be, we must never settle for what others may have put on us or make one circumstance in our lives become the benchmark for all others that come thereafter. We must never feel that "This is just the way I am. My mom was like this and I am too." We have a choice. You can choose to stay in the place where you are or you can make a different choice for yourself. If you choose to stay stuck in the negative space, you have chosen to keep the cap on your life. If you choose to move out of the negative space, your cap can be removed and you can move forward with defining your own way.

At times, it can be difficult to remove caps because sometimes we do not realize that we have one on. We may need to take some time to really think about what our cap is. Think for a moment about what has happened in your life that is holding you back. What is that one thing, person, or event that keeps you from striving to be all you can be? Once you discover what that one thing is, in order to move into new levels of possibilities, you must release it from your life. We must not allow circumstances to define our way, because each of us has the power to define our lives for ourselves.

There are many women who have achieved because they did not allow their circumstances to define them. Here are just a few.

Terry McMillian, author of the best-selling novel *Waiting to Exhale,* is an example of a woman who did not allow lack of money to define her. McMillan wrote her first book while struggling as a single mother and holding down a full-time job. You know how she did it? She woke up at five o'clock every morning to write. She spent the first moments every morning before the sunrise to work on her dream. She then got dressed, got her son dressed and ready, got him off to school, and spent her train ride to and from work editing her book. Terry McMillan is definitely a woman who was determined to make it, and she *did*! She did not let lack of finances, lack of time, or lack of resources stop her from fulfilling her dreams. Neither should you!

Oprah Winfrey is another example of a woman who has not allowed what other people have said or done in the past to define her. Raped by a family member, pregnant as a teen, being told that a woman who looks like her would never make it on TV, Oprah faced a number of circumstances that might have caused the average person to give up. Yet Oprah did not let her circumstances hold her back; she stepped over every obstacle. She removed every cap and was able to become all that she was meant to be. Now look at her go!

Don't let where you come from define you. I, too, came against a potential cap. Mine was being from a socioeconomically disadvantage community, better known as "the 'hood." The paths for escape from the 'hood seem to be limited to finding a means to "get rich quick" and move out. The desire to get money is what makes drug dealing so appealing for those who long for the instant gratification and material things that the drug dealer lifestyle can provide. Getting money any way you can is often thought of as the only way out of the 'hood rather than getting a good education or having a successful career. In my experience, when you are living in the 'hood, not too often do you have folks say to you "education is your ticket out" or "becoming successful in your career is the way to make a better life for yourself." Sometimes, even if you do have someone who encourages you to value education and legitimate employment, seeing the picture of fancy cars and other material things, better known as "bling bling," in the neighborhood or seeing images on music videos make that lifestyle seem much more appealing. As a result, young people may find themselves seeking to imitate the Biggie Smalls song that says, "Get Money!" by any means necessary.

For many in socioeconomically disadvantaged communities, or the projects, as Sister Souljah puts it, the creativity and the will to survive and to overcome horrible circumstances is usually destroyed because there are no "freedom spaces" where children can go to think and expand their minds beyond what they see in their 'hood. Physically escaping the 'hood is not even one-fourth of the battle anyway. Rather it is breaking the cycle of spiritual, emotional, intellectual, mental, and cultural death that even a brief stay in the 'hood can mean. It is struggling to understand basic concepts—such as who you are as an African American man or woman. It is discovering the relationship between your talents and skills and business. It is discovering how and where to get information when none seems available.[1]

I believe these challenges have led to the growing dominance of gangs and drugs in today's urban communities, which in turn creates a cap for many growing up in the 'hood. I had to work really hard to keep the 'hood cap off of me. Little did I know that I was in a fight for my spiritual, emotional, intellectual, mental, and cultural existence and found myself yearning to get out of my neighborhood. Unfortunately, my 'hood in Inglewood, and my overall community of South Central Los Angeles, did not provide a place that would help me to grow beyond my four corners. But I was blessed to have parents who valued education, who sacrificed to put me in a private school, where I met friends who exposed me to things that I never could have gotten in my community. My parents also put me in a YMCA summer camp, where I met my mentor when I was twelve years old, who also helped nurture my thirst for intellectual growth. My mother undergirded me spiritually by making me go to church every Sunday. I also learned to do for others by doing community service projects with my private school friends. I became aware that I could participate in making our world a better place, not only for me, but for those around me. These ingredients combined to make me look beyond the bling-bling mentality that so many little girls like me get caught up in. These ingredients allowed me to take off the cap that living in the 'hood could have placed on me. Instead, I wanted more for myself and for my community.

By no means do I intend to look down on anyone who may have a cap on her life. But I do encourage anyone who does to use the power within and the resources around you to remove your cap. For it is only in removing the cap that you can really discover your true power and purpose. So I am calling you to take off the cap that is holding you back and limiting your potential. It is time to take it off and wake up to the possibilities in your life!

REMOVE THE CAP

Before we go any further with creating your dream, we have to look a little deeper at what may be hindering your progress. We are always blaming something or someone for why we are not working toward our dream. So instead of acting like we don't see the "white elephant" in the room, let's start this process by acknowledging the things that may be keeping us "capped." What beliefs do you hold about yourself that are holding you back, that are putting a cap on your life? You see, beliefs are opinions we developed over time, formed by things that have happened in our lives. If we stop to examine the negative things we believe about ourselves and our circumstances, we can begin to understand why we have a certain belief system, whether negative or positive.

The key to changing negative beliefs about ourselves is to begin to see ourselves as God sees us. You see, God gave us the gift of life and gave us each gifts and talents to explore and share. God blessed us with unique personalities and purposes. No one else has the gifts that we each have. No one else can do what you do. But you must discover your gifts and be willing to use them. Your life is *your* gift—not your mother's, your mate's, your children's, nor your father's. God has placed in each of our hearts, minds, and bodies the power to fulfill our purpose. It is your life to create and to do as your heart desires but you can only unleash that power within if you take off your cap.

You may already know what your cap is, but you may not have figured out how to remove it. Up to this point, you may have never even acknowledged that you have a cap. This is why I call it the white elephant in the room. You know that one thing that everyone sees but no one wants to talk about? Well, that's the white elephant and it is time to acknowledge the influence it has had up to this point in limiting your becoming all that you can be. Whether you realize it or not, this roadblock, this cap has become your definition of yourself, your life, and it influences every decision you make. This cap wants you to believe that it is who you are really are, when really *it is not!*

You may be wondering how to remove your cap. Don't worry! I have developed a three-step process for cap removal: awareness, choice, and change. Let's explore each step in detail.

Cap Removal Step 1: Awareness

The first step in the cap removal process is awareness. Awareness is simply the act of discovering what may be holding you back. It is simply knowing what is stopping you, being mindful of the negative things you believe about yourself placed on you by other people or circumstances. Whatever it is, you must be aware of your cap. You must ask yourself what is capping you.

- Is it that you don't have any money to start your own business now?

- Is it that your man left you alone with the kids?

- Is it that you don't feel pretty enough or smart enough?

- Is it that you feel that you have more important things to do?

- Do you feel that your dream is impossible?

- Has someone asked you who you think you are, trying to make something of yourself?

- Do you believe that nothing in your life will ever change?

- Do you believe that you will never be anything because of what someone else did to you?

Whatever it is, call your cap into awareness. It may help you to list your cap(s) below.

My cap is or my caps are:

By calling attention to your cap, you are actually calling it into your awareness not just to name it, but to stop and think about how it affects your memories, emotions, thoughts, and dreams.

Cap Removal Step 2: Choice

The second step in the cap removal process is choice. You cannot change what has happened in your past, but you can choose a better future for yourself. You can choose to believe the best about yourself and your future. You can choose not to believe your cap and instead believe what lies ahead. The dreams of your heart often get filtered by your cap. If you've been told that you would never amount to anything, it could be that every time God places a dream within your heart, you are kept from fulfilling the dream because you continue to place a cap on it by believing the naysayer or the things that have happened to you in the past. But ultimately it is your choice to change that filter, to believe differently about yourself, to believe in yourself, and to remove the cap.

Cap Removal Step 3: Change

The final step in the cap removal process is change. Once you are aware of what is capping you and you have chosen to follow your heart's desire instead of your cap, then you are ready for change. In his book entitled *Taming Your Gremlin*, author and psychotherapist Rick Carson paraphrases the Zen theory of change:

> *"I free myself not by trying to be free,*
> *but by simply noticing how I am imprisoning myself*
> *in the very moment I am imprisoning myself."*[2]

A story in chapter 19 of the Old Testament book of Genesis will help us illustrate this third cap removal step. You may remember the story of Lot, the man whose family was instructed by God to flee their city so that they could avoid being destroyed during God's judgment on Sodom and Gomorrah. Lot's family was instructed to leave and not look back. Well, the family did flee, but one member of the family, Lot's wife, made the mistake of looking back: "But Lot's wife looked back, and she was turned into a pillar of salt" (Gen. 19:26 NKJ).

The main point I make here is that we each have a choice in life. We can either choose to look forward and take off our caps or be hindered by our past by looking back. In essence, when we look back we become like Lot's wife. We *stay stuck!* Lot's wife became stuck right in her tracks because she continued to focus on her past. She was stuck forever, looking at what was behind instead of focusing on her future of hope and possibilities that lay ahead.

We can never make it to where we want to go if we keep looking back. I wish Lot's wife had had the benefit of the Apostle Paul's instructions in Philippians 3:13–14: "Beloved, I do not consider that I have made it my own; but this one thing I do: forgetting what lies behind and straining forward to what lies ahead, I press on towards the goal for the prize of the heavenly call of God in Christ Jesus." Lot's story teaches us that when God brings change into our lives, we should move forward without looking back, or else we may never get where God wants us to go. God wants to bring you through, to bring you out even better, and to restore everything you have lost and more!

More Caps

I would love to be able to tell you that once you have completed the process of removing caps that you will be cap-free for the rest of your life. It is often stated that at every level there is a new devil. Well, that means that as you move forward in life, you will face additional caps. But if you use the same cap removal process of awareness, choice, and change, then you can overcome the caps you face at every level. Removing caps is an ongoing process. We must constantly challenge anyone or anything that seeks to limit us.

God does not determine your future by your past, so why should you? Our choice here is to *no longer* allow those caps to stop us. Instead we will work toward getting past them, fighting our negative self-talk as we continue on the journey to our dreams. If you can believe it, you will achieve it. If you can remain positive, then the positive energy will fight against the negative. If you can't stand strong enough, find a friend, sister, family member who will pull you back to your strength when you see you are weak *(we will talk more about this in chapter 6)*, so that you can make it. The important point here is to know that in order for us to continue to put the past behind us, we must consciously commit to the cap removal fight. There is no finish line in the race of achieving your dream. As you achieve one dream, there will always be a new dream to achieve. So know that caps will try and meet you along the way to limit how far you can go. You must find your own strategy to rise above them: stay on course, stay focused, and stay diligent until the end!

Now that you have discovered and are committed to removing the caps that keep you and your dreams bottled up, next you must discover what it is you want to do with your life.

WHAT IS IT THAT YOU WANT? WHAT IS YOUR DREAM?

Is it a better job or a new career? Is it a mate or a better relationship with the one you have? Maybe you dream of becoming a homeowner, losing weight, or going to college.

If your dream has to do with your career, your life's purpose, let me help you here. In the book *Do What You Are*, Paul Tieger and Barbara Barron-Tieger introduce the concept that there is an ideal job, or what I like to describe as a life purpose, for everyone! To find this, you must figure out what you would like to do and find the path that accommodates it. Therefore, the key to creating a future of your dreams lies in doing what you enjoy most! Tieger and Barron-Tieger say, "A few lucky people discover this secret early in life, but most of us are caught in a kind of psychological wrestling match, torn between what we think we *can* do, what we (or others) feel we *ought* to do, and what we think we *want* to do. Our advice? Concentrate instead on *who you are*, and the rest will fall into place."[3]

So who are you? Actually some of you may already know your gift and do not even realize that it is what you are already naturally good at doing. If you naturally love to do something and you are good at it, you have already discovered your gift. The fact that I can work on Imani, my nonprofit, all day and all night and never feel like I am working, indicates to me that I have found my gift. Sometimes I lose track of time because I love what I am doing so much. It is my desire that you find something similar for yourself.

If you can't figure it out on your own, I highly recommend Tieger and Barron-Tieger's book. Their process will help you discover how your personality type fits best with a particular career path. Gaining a better understanding of just who you are, what you are good at, what you like to do, and so forth, will *definitely* help define your calling, the first step in defining your way. Some of us are called to be teachers, preachers, entrepreneurs, hair stylists, counselors, designers, doctors, and lawyers. I encourage you to spend time exploring your calling or purpose.

After you have discovered your dream, your purpose, you must follow these instructions. Read them carefully, as they will help shape the rest of our journey together.

Write the vision;
make it plain on tablets,
so that a runner may read it. (Hab. 2:2)

Think about it. When you close your eyes and dream, what is it that you dream of doing, receiving, or becoming? When you have determined your answer to that question, take out a sheet of paper and write that dream in BIG BOLD letters across the top of that page. Putting your dreams on paper is an important step in defining your way. Take a poster board and some old magazine and cut and paste images and words that symbolize your dreams.

Yes, *stop* and *do it now!*

A more creative and visual way to write down your vision and your dreams is through a vision board. I have done a vision board, and it is amazing to see how the visions unfold. As a matter of fact, writing this book began as a vision that I placed on my vision board. Even though I had the vision, do you know how many times I doubted whether it was really possible? I thought, who are you to write this book? No one cares what you have to say. But guess what, I pushed through it to reach my dream. I reached my goal, and *so can you!* My goal in writing this book is for you to reach your goal. *So, you go, girl!!!*

PLOT YOUR PLAN

After you have written down your dream, you must next develop a plan for making that dream come true. When God told Noah to build the ark, he just couldn't up and start building; he needed a plan. But even before he could come up with his plan, like all of us he had to remove a number of caps that may have said: Man, you don't know how to build an ark! You are too old to be doing this! People will think you are crazy!

Despite these potential caps, Noah had to stay focused and make a plan to build the ark. He had to decide what to do to build the ark, in what order and how the work would be done. He had to make a plan in order to come to the finished product—the ark. Similarly, once you have written out your dreams, purpose, or vision—your ark—you must next develop a plan for how you will build it. This is what we will call your blueprint toward defining your own way. What things need to be in place for your dream to come true? Will you need to get additional education or training? What people will you need to meet? What will you need to do to "plan your work and work your plan"? This is the next step after you write your vision; you now must make it plain so that you can begin to work on obtaining it or running toward it. Even if you think you already know, do it anyway. Below, you will find space to write out your plan. It's right there. You have no excuse for not starting today. *Do not* put it off another day. *Stop here* and *do it now!*

MY PLAN

Within the next year, I would like to accomplish ...

Within the next five years, I would like to accomplish ...

EDUCATIONAL PLAN

What do I want/need to complete as far as education and training (for example, take a six-month course, apply to school, go to counseling with my mate, go to counseling for myself)?

What kind of help do I need to get started (school application, counseling appointment, etc.)?

What do I want/need to have completed to work toward my dream in the next five years (perhaps complete college or graduate school, become certified in my chosen field, save to buy a home)?

CAPS

The following caps may make it difficult for me to follow my plan (my kids, monetary issues, not having time to study, low self-esteem, etc.):

Here are some ways I will deal with my caps (for example, childcare or get up earlier every morning to study, cut back on these listed expenses, work on loving myself by looking in the mirror every morning and saying, "You are beautiful," etc.):

To download this form, see the Imani Life Transformations page at www.imani.org.

The purpose of creating this plan for yourself is to ensure that your goal becomes a reality so this long-term project will not be neglected. From this point forward, plan each day efficiently and plan each week effectively. Only then can you reach your goal.

One pitfall to avoid when planning out your work is procrastination. Do you ever find yourself saying things such as:

"One more day won't make a difference,"

"I can do this tomorrow," or

"I don't feel like doing this right now"?

If you find yourself uttering these or similar words on a consistent basis, you are either a procrastinator or you do not believe in yourself enough to obtain your dream. We will look at this unbelieving self spirit in our next chapter, but for now, I want to challenge you to push past those feelings and move on with working your plan. Start by replacing the preceding statements with these:

"Why put off until tomorrow,
what you can do today?"

"If you fail to plan, you plan to fail!"

Why do all this work? Because writing down each step you will need to reach your goal helps you to begin to create the blueprint for your dreams, just as Noah did for the ark. If your goal is to become a lawyer, what is that first step and each one thereafter? What are the steps necessary to become a teacher? A nurse? An author? Whatever it is, write down each and every action step you need to get there. If you do not know what you need to do to get there, find out what needs to be done, then do it! If you know anyone in this profession or craft, interview that person and get some insight regarding what you need to do. God has placed people in your reach to help you achieve your goals. All you have to do is ask them for help, information, and insight. If you do not know anyone in the profession, search on the Internet. (See the "Resource List" at the end of this book for additional Internet resources.)

◉

*Successful people turn everyone who can help
them into sometime mentors!*

—John Crosby

◉

*He [or she] who is afraid of asking
is ashamed of learning.*

—Danish Proverb

Since you have made it this far in this chapter it means you have decided to begin the process of letting go of your caps, you have created your vision board, and you have plotted your plan; so what's next?

IT'S TIME FOR A TEAM MEETING

A coach constructs with the team the plays it will use to win the game. Since I consider this book an instruction manual and I your coach, in the next chapters you will get a group of plays. And what is the point of the coach working with the team members to configure plays for the game? It is to win! The goal of any team is to win!! Just like a coach supplies plays for his or her team, my goal in supplying these various strategies and plays is for you to win the game of defining your own way. To win in the game of life!

Some of you will use all of the plays, some of you may use a combination; whatever it may be for you, I challenge you to complete the work of *definition* and exploration for yourself on the road to becoming the *best you* you can be!

Hut, hut, HIKE! Take off that cap and get out there and play the game of winning at your dreams.

*Success is to be measured not so much by the position
that one has reached in life as by the obstacles which
he has overcome while trying to succeed.*

—Booker T. Washington, *Up from Slavery*

⊠ ⊠ ⊠

DEFINING QUESTIONS

1. What kind of limits are you putting on yourself?

2. What cap(s) have you identified that you are wearing?

3. How will you move beyond your cap(s)?

4. What will you choose to believe about yourself?

5. What is your PLAN for your life?

6. What's your dream? Your purpose?

The E of Define

EDIFICATION

3

GET YOUR HOUSE IN ORDER

Anytime we know people are coming to visit, what is the first thing we do? We get our house in order! We go from room to room dusting, vacuuming, and getting things together. So why don't we apply this to our lives? If we are to reach our maximum potential in all areas of our lives, we must be sure that our house is in order. Getting our personal houses or ourselves in order may require us to do light cleaning, deep cleaning, or even some building and renovations. So the first E in DEFINE stands for *edification*, which means to build or uplift.

If we are to define our way and reach our maximum potential, we must get our house, ourselves, in order. If you want your dreams to come by and see you and stay for a while, girl, you have to make sure that the house where you want your dreams to dwell is in proper order. In this chapter, we will inspect our houses, in the areas of self-esteem, finances, health, and education, to see what building needs to take place. In order for us to reach our goal, our whole selves must be in order. Yes, it's time to get that life together! *Girl, get your house in order!* So let's get to work!

MIRROR, MIRROR ON THE WALL . . .

The first room we will work on is how you feel about YOU. When you look in the mirror, what do you see? If you do not like what you see reflecting back at you, it is time to take out a dust rag and remove all the negative thoughts and feelings about yourself. Let's take this negative self and call it our old self. When you put down this book, after having done all the exercises and the work to define self, our goal is to have a fresh start! Yes, once your negative thoughts and feelings are dusted off, your old self will be removed and you can have a fresh new start! In essence you will be a brand new you!

DON'T STAY STUCK IN THE PAST

Each of us has moments in life when we don't like something about ourselves. None of us is perfect, not even Halle Berry, Beyonce Knowles, or Oprah Winfrey. I am sure if you ask Halle, there are things about her looks that she does not like. Beyonce has things about her body that she does not like, and Oprah does too. Yet each of these women seems to be very accepting of themselves, flaws and all. Even though Oprah has had her continual struggles with weight, she still displays a high level of self-confidence and self-esteem. What makes the difference for these women? Oprah, Halle Berry, and Beyonce have chosen to lead with their strengths—their gifts and talents. They do not get stuck focusing on their negative attributes.

Which of your not-so-positive traits are you stuck on? Is it a personality trait? A physical characteristic? Something that happened in your past? Whatever it is, you have two choices if you want to get unstuck.

Choice #1:
You can do something to change it (provided it is changeable).
OR
Choice #2:
You can learn to love yourself exactly as you are, flaws and all.

Once you have decided what you are going to do about your negative trait or circumstance, then you can either focus on changing it or take your focus off it altogether. Whatever you do, don't get stuck in that place. The secret to the success of a number of well-known women is they keep their focus and don't stay stuck on negative situations or circumstances that happen along the way. Here are a few examples:

Tyra Banks: Many of us have heard Tyra's story about how hard it was for her as one of the few black women in the fashion industry when she first started. Tyra's early days in the modeling business were difficult, as she had to fight against racism. "No model should have to endure what I went through at 17," Banks told *Essence* magazine.[1] However, look at Tyra now. Tyra's fight in those early days gave her the opportunity to live out not just one dream by having a *fabulous* career in the fashion industry but to move on to her next dream of becoming a television producer. Tyra is an example of how to fight and not allow roadblocks from stopping you to live out your dream!

Vanessa L. Williams: In 1984, Vanessa Williams made history as she was crowned the first African American Miss America. However, do you remember what happened after she made history? Halfway into her reigning year as Miss America, the discovery of pornographic photos forced Vanessa to resign. She had been pressured into posing for the photographs that she had been

told would never appear in print, but in 1984 they came out in
Penthouse magazine.² The *Penthouse* scandal would have stopped
most women, but Vanessa did not let her past stop her. She had
a vision of what she wanted to achieve in life: to be a singer, actress, and Broadway performer. She did not let the controversy
stop her from living her dream. She has fulfilled her dream, in
part, because she did not become stuck in her setback. She overcame *all* of the critics and controversy and she is living her
dream—all because *she* believed she could make it and did not
look back!

Beyonce Knowles: Most people see Beyonce Knowles as always having been on top of the world, but she had bumps in her
road to success that could have kept her stuck. Rumors that surrounded her after the two original members of Destiny's Child
left were a subject of the tabloids. Most groups don't get past such
rumors; they usually stay stuck in the negative and break up and
quit. Beyonce didn't. She did not allow anyone or anything dis-
tract her from reaching her goals. Instead of getting stuck, she
turned those battle scars into one of the most inspirational of Destiny's Child's songs, "Survivor." Just look at a few lyrics from this
powerful song:

> You thought that I'd be weak without you
> But I'm stronger
> You thought that I'd be broke without you
> But I'm richer
> You thought that I'd be sad without you
> I laugh harder
> You thought I wouldn't grow without you
> Now I'm wiser
> Thought that I'd be helpless without you
> But I'm smarter

You thought that I'd be stressed without you
But I'm chillin'
You thought I wouldn't sell without you
Sold nine million
I'm a survivor,
I'm not gonna give up,
I'm not gonna stop,
I'm gonna work harder,
I'm a survivor,
I'm gonna make it,
I will survive,
Keep on survivin.'[3]

The most powerful part of this song I want you to take note of is "I'm a survivor, I'm not gonna give up, . . . I'm gonna work harder, . . . I'm gonna to make it"! Well, Ms. Beyonce overcame *all* of the critics and controversy and she is living her dream— because she believed it could happen in spite of it all. Actually, Beyonce Knowles, Tyra Banks, and Vanessa Williams are all survivors in their own right. None of these women got stuck in negative situations or circumstances. Their stories really speak to the importance of believing in yourself and your dream even when you cannot see the outcome anywhere in sight.

If you are stuck on seeing yourself as weak or not pretty or stupid, others will see you that way as well. When you see yourself as strong and pretty and smart, then others will see you that way, too! We can all be and will be survivors if we choose to. So what is your choice? Are you stuck on the fact that you can't lose that extra weight? Be like Mo'Nique or the actress Gabourey Sidibe from the movie *Precious* and love yourself curves and all. Are you stuck on the fact that your man left you and was cheating on you? He obviously could not appreciate the gift he had in you, so you are better off allowing a mate to find you who will appreciate you. Let's actually stay here for a moment.

Do you ever wonder why some woman find out that their man has been cheating or have any number of reasons for a really bad breakup and yet as soon as they leave one man, a good one comes along? Do you ever wonder why that happens to them and not to you? It happens because they *don't stay stuck!* They don't stay stuck hoping that their ex will get it together and come back. They don't stay stuck wallowing and thinking about all the things that they should, could or would have done. Instead, they believe in themselves and hold their head up high. They let go, believing in their desire to have a mate who appreciates them and who shares the desire to have a long, committed, and happy relationship. They may not know where this person is or when he will come, but they trust the desire to have better and *do not settle* for less. They believe in who they are and what they want, instead of focusing on what was lost. They are happily single and do not focus on finding a mate. They know that being single is not a bad thing and are happy with spending time with themselves. They are not like Lot's wife, who looked back and turned into a pillar of stone. Instead they look forward to possibility and promise.

God's desire for each of us is to live the life of our dreams. After all, it is God who plants the seed of desire and our gift in each of us. It is that desire that we can choose to nurture in the pursuit of reaching our dream. How do we nurture it? We nurture it by not giving up, remaining positive in the pursuit, and not staying stuck on the negative. Certain obstacles are often put in our path to hinder us from reaching our dream. We must honor the seed God planted in us by remaining focused, positive, and determined to make it to our dream.

Moving forward in any area of our lives is a choice we all have the opportunity to make. What will you choose? There may be some barriers that make this choice harder to make than others. However, we each have the power to fight against staying stuck on any obstacle that is put before us. We must choose to *fight*! Whether it's ole Jimmy, our weight, not having the money to go back to school, how we look, or how we feel about ourselves, we each have the power to choose. We can choose to *love* ourselves right where we are, and to fight, to be, and to have whatever we deserve. We cannot settle for less!

It is the choices we make that dictate the life that we live.

Every day presents opportunities to make choices. As we begin this new outlook on life, I want to challenge you to look at the choices you make. Consider whether you may be looking at yourself, your situation, your identity, your definition of yourself through the glasses of your past. If kept on, these glasses, will hinder the possibility of what you can see for yourself and your future. If you are looking at the present through the lenses of your past, you will *never* be able to see the future. You will stay stuck in where you have been, what has happened to you, and what others have said about you, instead of looking at possibility and working toward what you can be.

Often our negative self-image is produced by how things look through the lenses of the past, the caps that bottle our lives. These lenses produce a negative image that keeps you in a negative place and holds you back. These lenses keep you looking at things through your past and not your future! They have you singing about being defeated as opposed to being a survivor!! Those negative lenses influence how you feel on the inside, which then has an affect on what you accomplish, the kind of people you have in your life, and how you feel about yourself. But keep in mind Sidney Poitier's words: "You are not responsible for what has happened but for what you make of it." Ladies, it's time to set our past free!

It's time for you to inspect your stuck places. Complete the following chart to help you discover what negative feelings may be keeping you stuck. In the next column, write in how you would like to feel about this area. In the final column, take the time to write out what it will take for you to get there.

Since there is not much room on this page to do this, go to the Imani website and download this worksheet so you can have all the room you need to make new choices for the NEW YOU!

"HOW I FEEL ABOUT THIS"

How I feel about this:	Today	My new choice	What will it take for me to get to this choice
How I look			
My job			
My man or relationships			
My finances			
Other (fill it in)			

Download this form at the Imani Life Transformations page at www.imani.org.

Now go and take another look in that mirror and say to yourself, "I love you and we will get there!" Say this in the mirror every morning even when you don't feel like it. As you continue to plant the seed of this affirmation in your heart, soul, and mind, water it by repeating it over and over again. As you do, it will begin to grow. It will grow under the dirt, and eventually begin to sprout above the dirt. The children's book *The Carrot Seed* by Ruth Krauss helps to illustrate this growth process. In this story, a little boy plants a carrot seed. Neither his parents nor his big brother believed the carrot would grow. Despite that, every day the little boy pulled up the weeds around the carrot seed and sprinkled the ground with water, even though nothing came up. But then, one day, a carrot came up just as the little boy believed would happen.

The point of the story is that a seed does not grow overnight; it takes time and nurturing. This is called the law of seed-time and harvest. There is only a harvest after a seed is planted, nurtured, and watered until one day it grows into a harvest. Just like this story, if you plant a seed of self-love in your heart and continue to water it, that seed will eventually grow. From this point forward, commit to making sure that you water only positive seeds. Stop planting and watering negative seeds. Do not speak any negative words from your mouth. You may not be ready yet to plant positive seeds, but if you begin by refraining from planting negative ones, that is a good start. Pretty soon, you will begin to plant the positive seeds. Then you will be on your way living in your *maximum* potential, and ain't no stopping you now! Beyonce's song "Survivor" is definitely what I call my theme song, as *I will not stop!* I invite you to sing my theme song with me now . . .

I'm a survivor,
I'm not gonna give up,
I'm not gonna stop,

I'm gonna work harder,
I'm a survivor,
I'm gonna make it,
I will survive,
Keep on survivin.'

Thank you, Ms. Beyonce!
OK, let's move to the next room in our house . . .

GET YOUR HAND OUT OF MY POCKET

"According to national figures, Black women
live longer and die poorer than any other segment
of the U.S. population."[4]

The next area you will need to clean out or rebuild is your finances. How are you spending your money? It amazes me how some of us women spend our money on clothes, nails, and hair, but are unable to pay our bills. What's the point of looking good if you have nothing to show for it? Do you own your home? Are you saving money? If not, ladies it's time to get your finances in order!

In their book *It's about the Money: How You Can Get out of Debt, Build Wealth and Achieve Your Financial Dreams*, Rev. Jesse L. Jackson Sr. and Jesse L. Jackson Jr. write that the need to get our finances straight dates back to the African American's transition from slavery to freedom. In addition to becoming physically emancipated, we also had to learn to become economically emancipated. While there has been great progress since then, African American women still struggle with poverty, powerlessness, and having few prospects.[5] Therefore, it is critical that we as African American women get our finances in order. It is time to learn to manage our money as well as break the cycle of poor financial habits that continue to plague many of us. Once we learn to manage our money we can then maximize the money that we work so hard to make. There are a number of examples of African American women who made the most of their money. Let's look at a few:

Oseola McCarty: After having to quit high school to care for her sick mother, McCarty washed clothes for seventy-five years, never earning more than $10 a bundle. And yet, by age eighty-seven she managed to save $280 thousand, $150 thousand of which she donated to the University of Southern Mississippi for a scholarship fund for students with financial need.

Madame C. J. Walker: The daughter of ex-slaves, orphaned at seven, working at ten, married at fourteen, and widowed with an infant daughter at twenty, Walker became American's first African American female millionaire by selling hair care products. She started her business with less than two dollars. That's right! This millionaire started her empire with less than enough money than it takes to buy a cup of coffee today.

Mary McLeod Bethune: Ms. Bethune founded the Daytona Normal and Industrial Institute for Negro Girls with a little more than two dollars. In fact, she raised money for the school by selling sweet potato pies. This two-dollar school later merged with Cookman Institute and became Bethune-Cookman College, a historically black college that still exists today.

These women started with what they had and made smart financial decisions that paid off in the long term. Let their lessons of sacrifice, motivation, patience, diligence, and discipline be a shining example for us today! If you make your money work for you, you too can fund your dreams.

MAKING OUR MONEY WORK FOR US

In order to make your money work for you, you must first examine your relationship to money. For some, spending is an addiction, and breaking the habit means really taking a look at why you spend. According to Marilyn French Hubbard, author of the book *Sisters Are Cashing In,* "Many women have a poor relationship with money because they do not have a good relationship with themselves. When they feel insecure, they put diamonds in their ears and gold chains around their necks. . . . They spend money to ease the pain of hurt feelings. . . . Feeling empty or unfilled is common among women. The reasons vary, but they all create identifiable patterns for how woman see money, what they do with money, and what they expect money to do for them. They see and use money as a substitute for the fulfillment that they want to have inside."[6] To make your money work for you, don't try to use money as a substitute for something else. A new outfit or car won't make you feel better. Those things only give a temporary high. Once you come off of that high, you will have to look for the next fix. This translates into your continuing to spend more and more to keep that high. The next time you find yourself getting ready to make an impulse purchase, ask yourself these questions: "Why do I want this?" "Do I really need this?" "Am I just trying to get a fix?" There is nothing wrong with wanting things; the problem is that we often buy what we do not need and cannot afford.

You can buy an occasional outfit and still save for a new home and retirement, too. But you must have a plan. According to the *Essence Magazine's Money & Investment Guide*[7] it's not what you make, it's what you keep.

Goal 1: Make a Budget

The first step to getting your financial house in order is to make a budget. A budget is a plan for how you will use the income you receive. It is a plan for how much you will spend and how much you will save. A budget allows you to organize and control your financial resources, set and realize goals, and decide in advance how your money will work for you. In order to prepare a budget, you must first know how much money you have coming in, or your income. Then, you must determine how much money you need to spend on bills—these are your expenses. The table on the following page will assist you in developing your own budget. Now let's write your budget.

Your budget will help you not overspend and will make sure that you are saving as well as planning for emergencies. By following a budget, you will control what you spend, be able to live within your means, and decrease the amount of stress you experience from paying bills. Even if you do not have enough income to pay your bills, having a budget will let you know what your shortfall is and determine what expenses can be cut or how much additional income you will need to make up the shortfall. Having a budget is essential to getting your finances in order.

Goal 2: Get Out of Debt

Next, you must get out of debt. In 1997, I set a goal to pay off all of my credit cards and, two years later, I was able to cut up all my credit cards. What a rewarding feeling it was for me to be out of debt!! Why is this so important? An unexpected expense, impulse shopping and other spontaneous spending, unexpected medical bills, loss of a job, and other financial responsibilities are the main reasons many people get into debt. But getting into debt is much easier and a lot more fun than getting out.

When you buy items on credit and you do not pay off the balance, you end up paying more for an item than you initially spent. Credit card companies make their money from the interest that adds up when you do not pay your credit card charges in full on a monthly basis. The longer you owe, the harder it becomes to pay the bill off. Over time, this kind of debt can do more damage to your

MONTHLY BUDGET

INCOME	AMOUNT per month
Wages/student loans if applicable	
Other income	
TOTAL AVAILABLE INCOME	

FIXED EXPENSES	AMOUNT per month
Rent/mortgage	
Car payment/public transportation	
Car insurance	
Home/renters insurance	
Student loans	
Tuition (if a student)	
Savings	
Other	
Other	
TOTAL FIXED EXPENSES	

FLEXIBLE EXPENSES	AMOUNT per month
Groceries/meal plan	
Eating out	
Clothing	
Entertainment (movies, etc.)	
Transportation/gas	
Car maintenance (oil change etc.)	
Telephone	
Electricity, gas, water	
Cell phone	
Cable	
Internet access	
Gym membership	
Savings (or payment on current debt)	
Other	
TOTAL FLEXIBLE EXPENSES	

TOTAL FLEXIBLE EXPENSES	
TOTAL FIXED EXPENSES	
TOTAL INCOME	
DIFFERENCE (WHAT IS LEFT OVER OR SHORTFALL)	

To download this form, see the Imani Life Transformations page at www.imani.org.

credit than you realize. This concept also applies to rent-to-own options available at some stores. Any time you have the option to pay something off over time, there is usually an interest rate attached.

To use credit wisely, you should seek to pay your balance in full every month. If you are not able to do so, then think twice about using your credit on nonessential items. That means think twice the next time to pull out your credit card to buy a new dress and pair of shoes for that party on Saturday night.

Here is some additional advice that will help get your debt under control:

1. First, figure out how much money you can afford to set aside each month to go toward paying off debt.

2. Next, make a list of what you owe in order of the highest interest rate first.

3. Then develop a repayment schedule. What will you pay off first? How much will you pay each month on each? If you have several cards, paying them off may take a little time, but hang in there. In the long run, it will be worth it.

4. Don't use your credit cards except for emergencies. What good is paying them off if you just keep on using them and running up the bill? Keep them for emergencies *only!*

5. Finally, once you pay off all your debt, get rid of all of your credit cards. You may wish to keep one for emergencies (such as an unexpected car repair).

Goal 3: Save for Emergencies

Third, it's important to set aside some money each month to cover emergencies. Emergencies do not include a new outfit or dinners out. Rather emergencies are those times when your car's brakes need repairing or you have a dental emergency or some other necessity that comes up unexpectedly. Having money set aside for these emergencies means that you will not go into debt to pay for them. While it takes some effort to save, in the long run it pays off.

Some of us follow our grandparents' habit of placing our savings under the mattress or in a cookie jar. The tendency to do this might be greater when the economy is poor; however, it is still better to put the money into a savings account where it can earn some interest (no matter how little). In case you don't know what interest is, let me explain.

Let's say that you put $100 in a savings account that earns 5 percent interest per year. After one year, the account is worth $105. You made $5 because you made 5 percent interest. The second year, the account will total about $110, the third year, about $116. Building interest benefits you the most over time so the sooner you start saving money, the better. Now you know what I mean when I say make your money work for you!

Goal 4: Buy a Home

The fourth step to getting our finances in order is to buy a house. Even though purchasing a home creates a debt, it also creates investment potential. When you are renting a house or an apartment, you are not investing in anything that will give you a return. Instead, you are giving your money away to the person who owns your apartment building. You are helping that person pay his or her mortgage and investing into his or her financial future rather than your own. But what if you could take that same money and invest it in something that you own? That is what becoming a homeowner is about. As an added bonus, you get to live in your investment. As your home continues to increase in value and as you pay down your mortgage, the amount of equity you have in your home increases. Another benefit of owning a home is that your mortgage interest and property taxes can be written off your income taxes, reducing the amount of income you must pay tax on.

Goal 5: Save For Retirement

Finally, you must save for retirement. You must save for retirement even if it is twenty, thirty, or even forty years away. This is because social security will not cover your bills. Most of us dream of living a lavish lifestyle when we retire, traveling at our leisure, and more, or we believe we will enjoy not having to get up every morning to go to work. If this is the case, how will you be able to live if you will not have the income to pay your bills? To ensure a comfortable retirement, you must start saving today.

According to the website 401K.org, experts estimate that you'll need at least 70 percent of your preretirement income to maintain the same standard of living once you stop working.[8] Many options exist for retirement savings. Your employer may offer a 401(k) or 403(b) plan. Your employer may also match some portion of what you put into that account, which means that you will be able to save even more than you contribute. You should definitely take advantage of retirement options offered by your employer. Other options for retirement savings include stocks and bonds, certificates of deposits (CDs), and individual retirement plans (IRAs). To learn about all of your options, I recommend that you speak to a financial advisor or someone at your local bank. Some churches even offer financial literacy classes that will allow you to explore available options for retirement planning. The key is to learn as much as possible so that you can make the best decision for your long-term savings and retirement goals.

Other Financial Goals

The goals listed in the preceding pages for getting your financial house in order are fairly broad. You may have others. These may include saving money for traveling, buying a new car, or investing in rental properties. Whatever your financial goals, they are in your reach if you begin to be smart with your money and make a plan rather than just spending. Wealth building requires motivation, patience, diligence, and discipline. You can have anything you want if you set realistic financial goals, have patience as you work toward them. and discipline yourself to stay on the path.

I have included the following worksheet to help you to begin setting your financial goals.

MY FINANCIAL GOAL-SETTING WORKSHEET

MY FINANCIAL GOALS ARE:	How much I will save to meet this goal.	The date I want to meet this goal by?	What will I do now to save for this goal?	What will I do by the end of every month to save for this goal?	What will I do by the end of the year to save for this goal?

To download this form, see the Imani Life Transformations page at www.imani.org.

Even after you have completed the worksheet and have set some general goals, I still recommend that you speak to a financial advisor or other expert. You may also take advantage of other reputable financial literacy courses. The key is to learn as much as possible so that you can make sound decisions about your money. Your ultimate goal should be to accumulate long-term savings and to have the money you will need to live the life you desire in retirement.

OK, are we ready to move to our next room? This one may be even harder . . .

PUT DOWN THAT TWINKIE

> *It is even more challenging for us to excel if we're*
> *not taking good care of our bodies and our minds.*
> *Think about the kind of food you're eating, when you*
> *last exercised, and when you had a health check up.*[9]
>
> —Bill Cosby and Alvin Poussaint

I remember watching an awards show and LL Cool J came out on stage with his newly worked out and buff body. He was looking mighty good! He commented on the speculations that had been going around that he was on steroids or some other performance enhancing drug. LL's response was, "You could look like this too if you'd stop sitting on that coach and put down that Twinkie." Truer words have never been spoken. I am not saying that we are all meant to have six-pack abs or a perfectly toned butt, though Lord knows, I wish I had one! But just as LL said, many of us need to "put down that Twinkie." Being healthy helps us to feel good and to live and perform at our best! So the next room we want to look at is health!

According to the World Health Organization, health "is a state of complete physical, mental, and social well-being and not merely the absence of disease or infirmity."[10] We have discussed mental health earlier in this chapter as we focused on how you feel about yourself. Social health will be discussed in chapter 6. In this portion of the book, we will limit our discussion to physical health, which is how we take care of our bodies. Taking care of our bodies is made up of four components: (1) healthy eating, (2) physical activity, (3) rest and relaxation, and (4) taking care of our temple.

Healthy Eating

What are you putting into your body? Do you load up on fast food? Do you eat junk food like potato chips, drink soda, or lots of candy? What do you think eating high-fat, highly processed foods is doing to your health? Do you eat because you love food or because your body needs it to survive? Do you eat to make yourself feel better or to give your body energy? While we often eat for enjoyment, the real purpose of food is to provide fuel for our bodies. Just as cars need gas for their engines to operate properly, our body needs fuel so that our muscles, organs, and minds can function properly. We should focus on eating to live and not as a way to get our grub on. You must choose to keep your engines running properly, healthily, and productively. Think of it this way: you are what you eat. Do you want to look like a big old greasy piece of fried chicken? OK, I had to laugh, as I am sure you chuckled at that notion too, because who looks like fried chicken? But when LL Cool J said, "Put down that Twinkie," he had a point. If we eat healthily, we produce a healthy engine, one that is pumped up and physically fit. It helps to brighten our mood and gives us the energy to do what we need to do. When we don't eat healthily, we can feel sluggish, lack energy and motivation, and experience dampened moods.

Let's look at it another way. People who own luxurious cars often use a higher grade of gasoline. If you think of yourself as a Pinto, then put in the cheap stuff, the junk like French fries and Twinkies. But if you are like me and consider yourself a Mercedes, then you can only put in the premium gasoline. Even if you don't feel like a Mercedes now, if you begin to treat your body like one, your engine will begin to work in tip-top shape.

Historically many African Americans have eaten a diet of soul food. These foods tend to be fried, barbecued, or covered with gravy. My favorites include macaroni and cheese and peach cobbler. You can still eat these types of foods in moderation and in small portions. There are some good foods that are part of a traditional African American diet, like collard greens and other leafy green vegetables, and beans, which are high in fiber, calcium, potassium, and other nutrients. What can make these bad is being cooked with added fat and salt. If we put more emphasis on fresh fruits and vegetables, lean meat, and seafood, we can drastically change our health as a community. We can bake instead of fry our foods. We can even consider growing fresh vegetables as many of our foreparents did. If you are like me and do not have a green thumb or do not desire to grow your own fresh foods, other options for fresh produce include farmers markets, community gardens, food co-ops, and food bank programs. Focus on adding fresh fruits and vegetables to your diet as well as looking at the types of food you eat and how they are cooked.[11]

In addition to watching what you eat, you should also watch what you drink. A dentist once told me that drinking soda is like putting your teeth into a glass of acid and watching it degenerate. If that is what soda can do to your teeth, what do you think that it can do to the inside of your body? Many women wonder why they have such poor skin. Often this problem can be traced to drinking soda. You would be surprised to find how much sugar is in soda. Just curbing your soda intake can drastically change your health. Substituting water for soda is a small adjustment that will change how you feel. Drinking water is good for your health. Your body needs water to keep its temperature in order and to provide a way for nutrients to travel throughout your body. Water transports oxygen to your cells, removes waste, and protects your joints and organs. Your body needs water to survive.

If you need help with food preparation and learning what foods are best for you, there are many ways to get the information that you need. There are a number of cookbooks that can help you prepare food that is both healthy and tasty. I recommend Patti LaBelle's healthy cookbook titled *Patti LaBelle's Lite Cuisine*. Bob Green (Oprah's trainer) wrote a book called *The Best Life Diet*. You might also consider enrolling in a healthy eating or food preparation class at a local community college.

Obesity and the sicknesses it causes is a new form of enslavement for many African Americans. According to health and nutrition consultant Makeisha Lee, "We are losing our women in record numbers to easily preventable diseases such as heart disease, diabetes, and more; most of which comes as a direct result of obesity."[12] The Center for Disease Control and Prevention (CDC) estimates that an astonishing 53 percent of black women are obese, not moderately overweight, but obese![13] So let's do something about it! The point here is to take care of your body by looking at what you are putting into it. We can liberate ourselves by eating to live as opposed to living to eat.

Physical Activity

> *The evidence is overwhelming. Of all the choices we can make to stay healthy, the decision to exercise regularly may be the most important. An estimated 250,000 deaths each year occur due to lack of regular physical activity.*[14]

—Jeffrey A. Jacqmein, MD

Exercise or physical activity (I prefer this term to exercise since many people *hate* to exercise) is important not just to maintaining a healthy weight but it is also necessary fuel for the heart. Physical activity helps you to gain energy to help you perform better during your day. It reduces stress as well as produces chemicals called endorphins that foster an overall good feeling. Physical activity can help you sleep better, increase self-esteem, and maintain a healthy weight. As a matter of fact, exercising to maintain a healthy weight decreases a person's risk of developing certain diseases, like Type 2 diabetes and high blood pressure.

If engaging in physical activities has so many benefits, why aren't you exercising?

Well, many people do not exercise because they believe they do not have time or that it's not fun. The key is to find the right physical activity for you! Whether it's getting a gym membership or starting a walking club with your girlfriends, get moving. You can even include your family members after dinner in a game of basketball, bike riding, playing tennis, or running around the track at the local high school. All you need to do is find something that increases your heart rate that you actually like doing, and do it! If you choose something that you enjoy and people you enjoy it with, you are more likely to stick to it. And if you stick to it, you are more likely to see results.

Rest and Relaxation

Even God took a day off to rest, so what makes you think you don't need to!? Our cell phones need to be charged, car batteries need to be replaced, we gas up our engines and power up our laptops. So what makes you think you can just go and go without charging your battery? Rest or sleep, like diet and exercise, is important for our minds and bodies to function normally. In fact, according to the National Institutes of Health, sleep appears to be required for survival. Rats deprived of sleep die within two to three weeks.[15]

Sleeping is important to rejuvenate our body on a daily basis; it is something that we should not take lightly. When we are sleep deprived, we do not function at our best, we lack concentration and our mood and productivity are negatively affected. If you have problems sleeping, consider seeing a doctor. You may be suffering from a sleeping disorder. Snoring or having pauses in breath during sleep could be caused by something called sleep apnea. These sleep disorders could be the cause of your not getting adequate sleep.

In addition to getting enough sleep, as busy women we must take time out for our bodies to be replenished. Every evening from 9:00 to 11:00 and all day on most Sundays, I schedule Nicole time. This is when I take time to restore, replenish, rest, and relax. Sometimes that means soaking in a hot bath, reading a book, or just napping on the couch. You, too, must find some me-time. Find time to rest, relax, and restore yourself and replenish your body's energy levels.

TAKING CARE OF YOUR TEMPLE

"Or do you not know that your body is the temple
of the Holy Spirit who is in you . . ."

—1 Cor. 6:19a NKJ

When you hear the word temple, what do you think of? I think of something sacred, special, an edifice. So if I hold myself and respect my body as a temple, would I not take greater pride and be much more selective in the decisions that I make that will ultimate affect its upkeep? If this is the case, why do some of us not take pride in what we put into it when we eat, how we take care of it by exercise, who we allow to become one with us by having sex?

Keeping sex sacred and special is an even further need as AIDS is running rampant in the African American community.

Why are we as African American women a population with the greatest health disparities? How can we take more control of our total well-being? The first step is by getting informed about it. Let's look at our overall health.

According to the U.S. Department of Health and Human Services, the major health problems for African American women include heart disease, cancer, diabetes, kidney disease, vision loss, tuberculosis (TB), and sexually transmitted diseases (STDs), including HIV/AIDS. African Americans are about twice as likely to have diabetes as whites of the same age and are more likely to have serious health problems caused by diabetes. African American women are also disproportionately represented in the area of sexually transmitted diseases. Two out of three women who make up new cases of HIV are African American. In fact, AIDS is the leading cause of death among African American women ages twenty-five to forty. High rates of STDs, including chlamydia, gonorrhea, and syphilis are a problem as well. Even further, African American women are less likely to receive health care for many diseases, and when we do, we are more likely to receive that care after the disease has progressed significantly.

The following health statistics on African American women and men further highlights our need to engage in taking better care of our temples:[16]

- African American women are more than twenty-one times as likely to die from HIV/AIDS as non-Hispanic white women.

- African American women are more likely than all other women to die from breast cancer.

- Tumors are found in African American women at a later, more advanced, stage when there are fewer treatment options. Some reasons for this may include not being able to get health care or not following up after getting abnormal test results. Other reasons may include distrust of the health care system, the belief that mammograms are not needed, or not having insurance.

- African American women are 35 percent more likely than non-Hispanic white women to die from heart disease. Diabetes, high blood pressure, high cholesterol, lack of exercise, and smoking all put women at risk for heart disease.

- Studies have shown that African Americans don't get the same care for heart disease as whites because they don't get the same tests and treatments.

- Among people born in the United States, African Americans have the highest rate of tuberculosis (TB) cases, compared to other groups. African Americans accounted for almost 45 percent of TB cases in this country and 19 percent of all TB cases.

- Glaucoma is one of the leading causes of blindness in African Americans. African Americans are almost three times more likely to develop visual impairment due to glaucoma than other ethnic groups. But if glaucoma is found and treated early, it can often be slowed and major vision loss can be delayed. African Americans over age forty should get a comprehensive dilated eye exam at least once every two years.

- More than twenty-five diseases are spread through sex. Some STDs seem to affect certain groups more than others. African Americans have higher rates of Chlamydia, gonorrhea, syphilis, and herpes than whites. STDs are more easily passed from men to women. And many STDs have no symptoms. If you're having sex, get tested for STDs.

Given these grueling statistics, we must care enough to do what it takes to take care of our temple. The following are some steps even young women can take to better care from their temples:

- Get annual checkups. Getting annual checkups is important for your overall health. Just as you get oil changes, tires rotations, and tune-ups for your car, allowing a doctor to determine if all your parts are in working order is equally if not more important. Your doctor can find out if you are predisposed to certain conditions based on your family history and can recommend some preventive measures. It is easier for doctor address any issues earlier rather than later. So, if you have not had a recent physical examination, considering making your appointment to go today!

- Look at the types of food you are eating and engage in physical activity regularly. Making better choices about the food you eat can help prevent certain health conditions. Remember LL Cool J's advice: Put down that Twinkie. Healthy eating, combined with exercise, is a vital part of temple care.

- Rest and relax. Once again, rest and relaxation are both vital to optimal health. Be sure to recharge your battery on a regular basis.

- Let's talk about SEX. Another essential aspect of temple care is our sexuality. Sex is a difficult topic for some African American women to discuss, which may be why so many of us are suffering from unhealthy sexual attitudes and engage in unhealthy sexual practices. We are dying, ladies, from lack of knowledge and wise choices. We must talk about making better decisions about our sexuality if we are going to be empowered to make healthier life choices. The U.S.

Department of Health and Human Services has developed the ABCs of STDs (sexually transmitted disease).[17] Putting these into practice can help keep you safe and healthy:

A is for Abstinence. Refraining from engaging in sex of any kind (vaginal, anal, or oral sex) is the only 100 percent effective way to avoid getting an STD.

B stands for Be faithful. Being in a sexual relationship with only one partner who is free of an STD and who is also faithful to you limits the chance of infections.

C is for Condoms. If you are having sex, use a latex condom. Latex condoms have been proven to reduce the risk of HIV and other STDS, but only if they are used correctly and consistently every time you have sex.

Ladies, we must take control of our own health destiny by making healthy choices about our own bodies. We must say "no" when we need to, take better care of and take pride in the temple that God has given us! It's time to release the shackles that produce unhealthy habits that affect our bodies, minds, and spirits—our temples. It is time to live productive lives!

GET YOURSELF A PASSPORT

Education is our passport to the future, for tomorrow belongs to the people who prepare for it today.[18]

—Malcom X

The final area you will need to build upon if you are going to define your way is getting an education. Our ancestors were denied the right to an education when they were slaves. Most of the masters did not permit their slaves to read as they believed reading brought ideas and those ideas would then lead to discontent, which would ultimately lead to revolt. To keep the slaves in line, they denied them education.

Once freed, our ancestors took getting an education very seriously. After emancipation, African Americans' place in society was not defined by how much they knew, but by how little they knew. So as they began their lives as free people of color, they realized that education provided the opportunity to make a better life as free people. They realized that "education provided the most direct path out of poverty for a people left impoverished and mostly illiterate after emancipation. Education has been the core of our people's progress. Without education to lift us up, most of us would still be struggling at the fringes of society."[19] The fact that the slave masters would not allow their subjects to read or write should tell us something. The slave masters knew that keeping slaves mentally enslaved was just as important as keeping them physically enslaved. Being uneducated keeps a person trapped mentally and physically. That is why Malcolm X calls education a passport, because it can take you places. For our ancestors, education became the passport to better jobs, better homes, better opportunities, and thus better futures. It allowed them to sit at the table where negotiations, decisions, and progress were taking place.

But do today's black youth take their foreparents' struggles for granted?

◉

Given this glorious history, it troubles us that so many black youth are as thrilled about getting an education as they are about getting head lice."

—Bill Cosby and Alvin Poussaint.[20]

Like them, when I look at us today, when I see the state of current black America, the glamorization of the drug dealer and the high school dropout rate, I am frightened to see that, despite how far many of us have come, too many of us are standing still. Many of us are prioritizing living a lavish lifestyle over getting a quality education. We want to live in the BIG HOUSE and live the lavish lifestyle without paying the price to get there. We must understand that the fast way to owning a big house of our own may also be a way of feeding into the future downward spiral of our people. Why is it that our ancestors fought so hard for us to have hope and opportunity, but many of us today do not reach out and grab it? Unfortunately, many remain mentally enslaved by not understanding the value of education.

For many of us, ignorance has, indeed, become bliss. We are more concerned about what we wear and drive than we are about how we grow intellectually. Has this become our modern day shackle? The attraction of living in the big house and driving the big fancy cars may also be a product of what our ancestors could not have as slaves. It is an immediate solution for a long-term desire that keeps you stuck in an "I want it all now" mentality. Becoming an actress, basketball player, or singer is also glorified as an easy way to the glamorous life, but what happens when someone makes it in those careers and gets hurt and can no longer play or something happens to a singer's vocal chords and he or she can no longer sing? Or what happens when you do not have a great business mind or you did not study business or obtain your college degree?

Well, I'll tell you what can happen. In a radio interview, Mary J. Blige said she wishes she had taken business courses in college so that she could understand when her lawyers, agents, and managers are negotiating deals on her behalf. Your agents, managers, and lawyers, with their college degrees, can negotiate a deal to make sure they get paid while you may not even be able to understand what is going on all because you lack the proper education.

What about the plight of our elders? Many of us take for granted that our elders pushed and fought so that we can get the educational opportunities they did not have. My own experience is an example. Now that I have obtained my degree, it still pains me to watch my mother struggle, a woman who has worked in her profession for more than thirty years, in which she has expertise and is competent. Yet young college-degree holders enter her career at a higher pay scale and get promoted over her because my mother does not have that four-year college degree. If my mother had been given the opportunity to get a passport, her burden might have been lighter.

When I speak of education, I am not just talking about an undergraduate college degree. There are many education paths that a person can take, including community college, trade schools, and cosmetology schools. Any educational opportunity that will allow you to advance in your career is a passport.

In his first State of the Union Address to Congress in February 2009, President Barack Obama said the following about education:

> In a global economy where the most valuable skill you can sell is your knowledge, a good education is no longer just a pathway to opportunity—it is a prerequisite. . . . And yet, . . . we have one of the highest high school dropout rates of any industrialized nation. And half of the students who begin college never finish. This is a prescription for economic decline. . . . I ask every American to commit to at least one year or more of higher education or career training. This can be community college or a four-year school; vocational training or an apprenticeship. But every American will need to get more than a high school diploma. And dropping out of high school is no

longer an option. It's not just quitting on yourself, it's quitting on your country."[21]

Education does not stop with whatever degree or certificate you earn. Education is a lifelong process. To truly succeed, you must invest in lifelong learning, which means finding information and resources that will help move you farther along your journey to define yourself and be all that you can be. Always keep a zeal for learning, even when you are not taking a class or making a grade. Intelligence, curiosity, passion, motivation, intuition, making smart choices and valuable judgments go hand in hand with your education. Reading newspapers and magazines helps keep you on top of current events and inspires thoughts and ideas. Joining clubs and organizations that fit with your interests will allow you to continuously grow in your field and interact with people who are willing to share their knowledge and experience. One line I remember from the movie *The Great Debaters* goes like this:

"We do what we have to do so we can do what we want to do."[22]

Or we do what we have to do so we can get where we want to go. Or we do what we have to do so we can be what we want to be. Part of that process should be to continuously educate yourself.

Education is a passport to gaining information and skills that will be used for the rest of your life, no matter where you go or where you work. Education gives you the ability to express your thoughts clearly in speech and in writing. It gives you an avenue to grasp intangible concepts as well as increase your understanding of what is going on in the world. There is nothing better than to have an avenue to explore your curiosity and to have a place where your thoughts and ideas can be conceptualized. Nothing can do that better than to flex your brain muscles through reading, writing, and all of the exploration that education definitely brings.

Even further, education gives a competitive advantage. Experts at the University of Texas who have researched the performance and job success of college graduates and have concluded that, nationwide, college graduates with a bachelor's degree earn about 80 percent more per year than those who only complete high school. In fact, those whose education stops with a high school diploma may see their wages decline over time.[23]

As you leave this chapter, I hope that you will use the tools to begin to build a definition of yourself that includes someone who holds herself in high esteem, uses money wisely, takes care of her health, and pursues education. These are, indeed, essential to getting your house in order.

⌧ ⌧ ⌧

DEFINING QUESTIONS

1. How will you begin to make your money work for you instead of you always having to work for money?

2. What financial goals have you set for yourself?

3. How will you take better care of your body?

4. How will you make healthier choices about what you eat?

5. How will you add some form of exercise to your life?

6. How will you find time to relax and rejuvenate?

7. What education do you need to take you to the next level?

4

YOU ARE A GIFT

*Dress gives one the outward sign from
which people can judge the inward state of mind.
One they can see . . . the other they cannot.*

—Queen of England writing to the Prince of Wales

In the previous chapter, we focused on edifying the inside of the house—who we are, how we feel, what we have and how we utilize what we have to work toward DEFINING our way. In this chapter, we will focus on the outside of the house.

Have you ever seen a house that needs a paint job on the outside? It doesn't matter to you how that house is laid out on the inside, you will make certain assumptions about the inside based on how the outside looks. The same is true with gifts that you receive. It doesn't matter how wonderful the gift is; if the packaging is raggedy you may not even want to open it. When you are celebrating a birthday, Christmas, or any other festive occasion, which gift do you choose to open first? Even before you touch it or shake it, you look at the wrapping. If the paper is all tattered and torn, are you as excited about the gift inside? Probably not. Well you, too, are a gift. And, like any other gift, the first part of you anyone experiences is how you are packaged. Unfortunately, you never get a second chance to make a first impression. Your first impression is made even before you utter a word based solely on your packaging. This chapter will look at your appearance, your gift wrapping, and the impact it has on how people first experience you.

Have you ever thought about what your clothes say about you? Do they say you have good sense and good taste? Do your clothes say you respect yourself and that you expect that same respect from others? Do you take enough time in the morning to properly groom yourself, making sure your hair is nice and neat and your clothes are ironed and neatly put together? How do you present yourself to the world?

It is human nature for people to make assumptions about you based solely on appearance and dress. The good news is you have the power to influence what others' first assumptions about you will be. Regardless of your level of income, social position, education, or status, you can take the time to ensure that your outward appearance is a reflection of the opinion you wish for others to have of you when they see you. This, like all other discussions we have had up to this point, is a matter of choice. The choice is yours. Yes, only you can determine whether the world will view you as sloppy or well put together. You can choose to take the time to do what is needed to practice good hygiene. You can select clothing that lines up your wardrobe with the image you wish to create for your life. I've heard it said that you should not dress for the job you have but the job you want to have. You are a gift, so wrap yourself well and give time to how you put yourself together. For often our outer package reflects how we feel about ourselves inside. Therefore, self-esteem is a key contributor to your packaging.

SELF-IMAGE IS CONNECTED TO SELF-ESTEEM

Self-esteem focuses on how you feel about yourself; self-image focuses on how you see yourself and how you want others to see you. Because the two go hand in hand, it is important that you focus on both. It makes no sense to feel good on the inside and not display it outside, and vice versa. It is important that *we define how we wish to feel about ourselves and the impression we wish to make on others.* We should not allow our image to be defined by others in ways that we do not want or do not like. Self-esteem and self-image combined lead to our feeling good and looking good at the same time. My mantra about self image is:

Life is a gift, so wrap yourself well.

Since we now know that our self-esteem is tied to how we put ourselves together, if we are not happy with ourselves, we will not take the time to make sure the picture we give to the world is a positive one. According to Dr. Joe Rubino, a person's self image is the *mental* picture that depicts not only details that are potentially available to objective investigation by others (height, weight, hair color, gender, I.Q. score, and so on), but also items that have been learned by that person about himself or herself, either from personal experiences or by internalizing the judgments of others.[1] Therefore, your image has to do with how you see yourself as well as how people perceive you, which then affects how they relate to, work with, or respect you. In essence, self-image affects whether people will relate to you positively or negatively, which in turn has a significant effect on your self-esteem. Think about it. If people are interacting with you negatively merely by first impression, how does that make you feel good about yourself? That is why it's important for you take strides that will help them see you in a positive light.

Let me state clearly that looking good on the outside has nothing to do with designer labels such as Donna Karan, Prada, Jimmy Choo, Gucci, or Coach. A person can look just as good in Wal-Mart and Target clothes as in designer duds. The key here is to find a look that works for *you*. Keep in mind, if you choose to shop at discount stores, you can shop cheap but you do not want to look cheap. So if you see a look in a magazine you really like, search for a cheaper version in a discount store. There are also all kinds of magazines and television shows that show you how to shop cheap but not look cheap, including my personal favorite, The Style Network's *The Look for Less*. It is possible to enhance your wardrobe without going into debt. For example, purchasing a few key pieces that you can mix and match is a resourceful way to create a full and versatile wardrobe without spending too much money. You do not have to sacrifice your financial goals in order to dress well.

A key to proper packaging is ensuring that the clothes you choose are appropriate for your body type. Not everyone can wear everything, but there are some things that can flatter every body type. Your height, weight, and build determine which styles you should wear and which ones you should avoid. If you are not a shopaholic like I am or you are not good at figuring out what clothing is right for your body type, consider finding someone whose image you admire and might want to emulate and who shares your general body type.

My image role model is Diahann Carroll. For those of you who know Diahann Carroll, I am sure you will agree that, like First Lady Michelle Obama, Diahann is a woman who epitomizes style and grace, sophistication and elegance, and is always impeccably dressed. Because I admire the way she puts herself together and how she carries and expresses herself, she became a model of the image I wished to portray. When I was a little girl, I wanted to be just like Diahann Carroll, based on the power, beauty, and respect she commanded just by her mere presence. Oprah Winfrey is another woman whose images I admire. Like me, Oprah is a woman with curves; she runs her own businesses and is respected for being business-minded. When Oprah enters a boardroom or is seen on television, she is always neatly and professionally dressed. She wears clothes that are becoming to her full figure. While I cannot afford the designer labels that Oprah wears, I can definitely recreate her look within my budget.

The final woman whose image I have used to create my own style is Halle Berry. I am mindful that some of Halle's attire, such as what she wears in movies or television, is not appropriate for the average woman. In her everyday clothes, however, Halle does not conform much to trends, and I see the pieces she wears as timeless. That raises a good point.

Keep in mind that what you see Halle, Rihanna, Beyonce, Tyra, Gabrielle Union, or J-Lo wearing on TV is not necessarily appropriate for you to wear. The venue they are wearing a given outfit in and the venue in which you would be wearing it may differ. If the two do not line up, you should not try and recreate that look. Even as you search for images to help you develop your own look, you must still keep in mind your body type. You must also keep in mind what is the appropriate attire in a particular setting. The key is to work toward an image you wish to give to the world and the vision you wish for others to perceive when they first experience you.

You have the power to make your own statement, your own self-definition. The first part of you that arrives in any room, whether it is a classroom or a boardroom, is your appearance. So take some time to focus on gift wrapping. Why do I call this gift wrapping? If you are flourishing, your house is in order, and you are working toward living the life of your dreams, part of this package is indeed the gift wrapping! Therefore, another key to ensuring proper packaging is making sure you are dressed in the right outfit at the right time. Think of the difference you make in meeting a potential employer wearing a suit and carrying a briefcase as opposed to wearing a lycra dress that is hugging your hips or is low-cut and too short. Do you see the difference in the two images? Wearing the lycra dress is obviously inappropriate to wear at a job interview, but even wearing it at a nightclub can present the wrong image to potentially interested men. It is within your power to choose to wear clothing that presents the image you wish to have for yourself whether you are in a nightclub, a board room, in the mall, or even at church.

If you don't believe a particular dress creates a certain impression, try people-watching for just thirty minutes at a mall or any other public place. As you watch people coming to and fro, take note of the first impression you form of each person based solely on how they are packaged. It is amazing how much information we can conjure up about a person based solely on how they are dressed.

Think for a moment about the image you wish to give to the world. Use the following chart to write your thoughts about what image you would like to portray.

What I Would Like People to See When I Arrive Is a Woman Who Is . . .

Now that you have determined what theme you want your image to project, think about how you will develop the image you have chosen. Let's call this theme the title of your play. Imagine that you are an actor, starring in the play of your life. Then, take a moment to create your wardrobe.

IF MY VENUE IS:	My wardrobe is:	What does this say about me?
Work/office		
Club/party		
Church		
Date or going to dinner		
Going to the gym		

To download this form, see the Imani Life Transformations page at www.imani.org.

I have completed an example below based on the image I chose to create as a program director in my twenties. My challenge was that I often went into agencies where I was significantly younger than my employees. The wardrobe I developed to meet this challenge looked like this:

IF MY VENUE IS:	My wardrobe is:	What does this say about me?
Work/office	*Suit or skirt with tasteful sweater or wrap dress*	*Professional Smart A woman who is in charge and knows what she's doing*

Even though most people in the nonprofit world dressed more casually, it was important to me as a young professional to portray a more professional image. I believed it added to my being taken seriously by my employees. If I had walked into the work environment wearing jeans and a T-shirt, I believed my image would have said that I was a young woman who was inexperienced and did not know what she was doing. Everyone may not have felt that way, but I believe that a significant portion of my staff would have. This is because jeans and a T-shirt give one image while a suit gives another. Wouldn't you agree? For me, wearing a T-shirt and jeans to work would have projected a youthful image, which could have resulted in it being difficult for me to command the respect that a successful supervisor needs. This, in turn, may have led to my employees being disrespectful and unwilling to follow my directions. Sure, I would have been just as smart in my jeans as I am in my suit, but if people perceive me as youthful and unprofessional, that is how they would have approached me and interacted with me.

That said, we will spend the remainder of this chapter providing a few "gift wrapping" tips as you design your fresh new wardrobe for your fresh new life.

Hair

My mother always said to me, "Do not go out of the house with that roller in your head!" I took that to heart and now use that as my guide for the idea that your hair should always look presentable because you never know who you will see when you walk out of the door. Therefore, take the time to make sure your hair is always neat, groomed, and combed. I remember Oprah telling Gail this exact same thing, telling her not to go out of the house looking like a "*shulmpadinka*." Never leave the house with your hair uncombed, not even to run a quick errand.

Be sure to keep your hair clean. Dirty hair smells in ways that no amount of perfume can hide. I recommend that you wash your hair at least once every two weeks. If you wear braids or other natural styles, you may be able to wait a little longer between washes.

If your hair is frizzy or you are prone to sweating in your hair, don't try and wear it down. Instead, a neat ponytail or bun or even a headband for those shorter styles always looks better than to try and wear your hair down when it looks a mess. Trust that if you can see those naps, so can everyone else!

Check your hair's roots. Nothing ruins a woman's look more than horrible-looking roots. If it is time for a perm or to twist your dreads or your braids are getting old, make an appointment to go and see your hairstylist. If you have to wait to make an appointment, wear a headband in the meantime.

Choose the right hairstyle for your industry. For example, if you are a chef, you will want to select a style that keeps you hair pulled up and away from food. On other hand, if you are a cosmetologist, you want to keep your hair in the latest styles. Who wants someone to do her hair who does not keep up with her own?

Make-up

You never want your face to arrive before you do. So don't wear so much make-up that this is all people see.

Make-up is designed to enhance, not replace. Eyeliner should not extend any further than your eye. If you want to look like an ancient Egyptian, then you are, for one, in the wrong century and on the wrong continent. While we are on the subject of liners, should you choose to wear lip liner, it should blend with the lip color you are wearing. Think: black eyeliner is only for your eyes, not your lips.

Again, makeup is intended to enhance your natural beauty not replace it. Remember this: *enhance, not replace!*

Details Matter

Pay attention to detail. The impression left by a great outfit can be ruined with scuffed shoes, a spot on a blouse, or even a missing button. Take the time to wipe or shine your shoes. Keep your clothes clean and learn how to sew on a simple button.

Stay fresh. Body odor is a no-no. You should not only look fresh, you should smell fresh, too. Don't forget to change your feminine hygiene products often during your menstrual cycle. And, by all means, don't forget to put on deodorant in the morning. Keep in mind the smell you want to arrive when you do should be from nothing other than your perfume or lotion of choice. That said, do not go overboard in using perfumes and lotions. There is nothing worse than too much perfume! There is such a thing as too much of a good thing!

Jewelry

Avoid wearing too much jewelry. A ring on every finger is not necessary.

Avoid wearing jewelry that is too flashy. You should be the focus of a person's attention, not your jewelry. Again, moderation is key!

Foot- and Legwear

Your shoes should always be darker than your stockings. Never wear pantyhose you know have holes or runs in them. If you are going to a job interview or other important event, consider carrying an extra pair of hose with you, just in case.

Keep your shoes in good repair. If your shoes are tapping like Savion Glover's, it might be time to get them repaired or replaced.

Do not ever wear *house* shoes outside of the house unless you are walking up your driveway to pick up your newspaper. They are called house shoes for a reason!

The Fit

Skirts and pants should not be so tight that they convey a message of sexuality. If this is the impression you wish to leave, why are you only interested in people experiencing that one side of you? You have much more to offer than your body.

Exposed cleavage and miniskirts are not appropriate attire if you want to be taken seriously. Even if you are at a nightclub, be mindful that a little cleavage says one thing; a whole lot says something altogether different. Again, be mindful of the setting. In some settings dressing a bit sexy may be appropriate, but never at work. You should make sure your clothes are the right size. If you have gained a little weight and you are still wearing clothes that are a size or two too small, it's time to let them go and get a larger size. Wearing improperly fitting clothing looks worse than finding the size that fits. The same is true for those who have lost a little weight.

GOT IMAGE? NOW WHAT?

Now that you are on your way to creating your image, how will you act and interact in ways that are in line with that image? Information on websites like coping.org will help you develop a script to go along with your new image. You must first develop expectations for how you are to act in any given situation as well as how you will react to others. So, if you act and react and dress according to the expectations, then you will develop high self-esteem. You cannot control how other people act, you can only control how you act and react. Once you have set certain expectations for how you will act, how other people act is not your concern.

You may be asking, how do the variables you choose for yourself interact with one another? Do your actions or reactions give off a positive or negative vibe? I can explain this further by utilizing a basic physics principle, Newton's third law, which says, "for every action, there is an equal and opposite reaction." In terms of our discussion, think of it this way: every action has a reaction. For instance, if someone forgets to put on deodorant, letting off a very specific smell, they definitely get a certain reaction, don't they? This according to Newton's law is a reaction based on an action; the action was forgetting to put on deodorant. Generally speaking, the choices you make about how you put yourself together have specific effects on others who interface with you. The choices you make about how you dress, act, and react all invoke a reaction. A reaction that you can choose to control regarding how others define you filters into how you feel about yourself and affects your self esteem.

Finally, to maintain positive self-image you must develop positive self-talk that reinforces that image. Positive self-talk produces positive self-affirming behaviors, just as negative self-talk produces self-defeating behavior.

Here are a few things that can help improve your self image:

- Change negative thoughts to positive thoughts by focusing on the positive aspects of your life rather than the negative ones. If someone says something negative to you, consider if any of what they have said is constructive and then toss the rest out. Don't let the negatives negatively affect your opinion about yourself.

- Note the positive comments that people have said about you. If you write them down, you can refer back to them when you are having one of those difficult days and/or a hard moment. This will help you remember who you truly are and put you back into your positive space.

- If you discover any changes that need to be made in terms of your clothing, appearance, hair style, or behavior, make those changes. Accept things about yourself that you cannot change and learn to think about them in a positive way. There are things we all have power over to work on, and others that are the way they are. We must learn the difference, change what we can, and love and learn to accept what we can't. If you do not know the difference, find a positive team member to help you (we will discuss this more in chapter 6).

- Don't be limited by your internal image; step outside of it and break free. It doesn't have to control you or keep you down. Acting differently will change how others see you and will also help to change your own attitude towards yourself and your abilities.[2]

Defining yourself includes building yourself up on the inside and the outside. Because the packaging is the first thing that people see, we have focused on it to ensure that your inner beauty shines through a beautiful package. It is my desire that your outer appearance not hinder you from that right business relationship, moving up in your job, getting accepted to the college of your dreams, or even your dream of meeting Mr. Right. As you define your way, remember that *life is a gift, so wrap it well!*

⊠　⊠　⊠

Defining Questions

1. Who is the person you want people to see when you enter the room? What is she like? What impression do you want her to leave?

2. In what ways do you have to alter your dress to reflect the impression you wish to leave?

3. What do you need to do transform your look so that it reflects the new you?

The F of Define

FAITH

· 5 ·

THE LAND OF CHOICE
Believe and Receive or Doubt and Do Without

Our thoughts determine our destiny.
Our destiny determines our legacy . . .
REMEMBER: You are today where your
thoughts have brought you. You will be tomorrow
where your thoughts take you.

—Rev. Run

Through the work you have done thus far while reading this book, you have defined your way in various aspects of your life: career, health and fitness, finances, how you put yourself together, and how the world sees and interacts with you. In so doing, you have explored where you are and where you wish to go. You have examined the labels others have put on you and chosen new labels for yourself.

Now that you have defined your way, you must choose to keep your eyes on the prize by believing your dreams are within reach.

So what will you choose?

Will you choose to believe in your dream?

Believe you can achieve and receive it.

Will you believe in your gift, your skills, your purpose?

Or will you doubt?

What will you choose for yourself from this day forward?

In order to keep your eyes on the prize of achieving a self-defined life, having faith is a must. Because doing something new can be scary, we must step out on faith to succeed. Whenever we are trying something new in life, we must muster up all the determination, assurance, trust, and confidence we can find to be successful. We must push past the fear and stay focused on what we want, where we are going, and the dream we wish to come to life. Once you have your plan in place and begin living out the dreams and goals you have defined for yourself, you must be willing to face and overcome the fear that often sets in. Faith is the key to overcoming the fear.

◎

Faith is the substance of things hoped for,
the evidence of things not seen.

—Heb. 11:1 (NKJ)

Some authors define faith in terms of the law of attraction. That is, your thoughts, emotions, beliefs, and actions, whether negative or positive, attract into your life matching people, circumstances, and experiences with similar thoughts, emotions, beliefs, and actions. Your life is a product of your beliefs. My pastor, Cecil L. "Chip" Murray, used to say that your attitude dictates your altitude. So in order to get where you strive to go, you must believe in the unique gifts that God has given to you; you must believe that by using those gifts, you can achieve the goals you have set for yourself. While you may have moments of doubt, you must not let those moments take you off your path. You must fight to keep the belief, trust, and happy assurance that you will achieve what you believe.

FAITH'S STARTING POINT

But where does this faith start? Faith begins with God, who uniquely gifts each of us with a special mission or purpose. If we believe that God loves each of us enough to give us our own unique gift, we must also believe that same God wants us to use those gifts to live out our purpose. Therefore, we must also believe it, so that we can achieve it and receive it. If we doubt, we will do without. To be ultimately successful, you must call on the power of the Almighty. It is God who has put the desires in our heart, and it is God who will help us to live out our purpose. Let's explore this issue of faith by examining a story from the Bible.

The Old Testament tells the story of the Israelites who walked through the wilderness to reach their promised land. But the clincher here is that they walked for forty years on what should have been an eleven-day trip. You might be wondering why it took so long for the Israelites to reach the promised land. Well, it took them so long to reach their destination because they did not have faith in the vision of the promised land. They believed that there was a promised land, but they just didn't exercise the faith on the path it took to get there. Not believing in the path also meant ultimately that they did not believe that God would bless them to see their dream become reality. Instead, they kept walking around the same mountain over and over again, because they could not see beyond where they were in order to get to where they were going. They did not keep their eyes on the prize and stay focused on their goal. Instead of focusing on where their faith could take them, they focused on the barren desert. They only believed what they could see, and all they could see was the wilderness in front of them.

Like the Israelites, many of us all find ourselves in the same circumstance, not being able to see beyond the wilderness of our lives. A wilderness is a barren, uninhabited land. It is desolate, destitute, and reeks of death. There are no people, no plants, no water, nothing. It is a place characterized by enormous empty space. The wilderness is a place that can cause you to doubt whether you have what it takes to make it through. The wilderness is a place that tests your ability to believe in what you cannot see. It is also often a plot of the Enemy to keep us from believing in our dream, to make us lose heart and give up.

If we want to avoid getting stuck in the wilderness of life, we must put our faith in God, which requires us to believe in what we cannot see. We must believe that no matter what is going on now, it is all working together for our good. Faith is to know that even if God does not deliver us from a bad situation, God will use the circumstance for our good. Instead of using the wilderness experience to deepen their faith, the children of Israel chose to complain about being in the wilderness. Rather than believing they would reach a land flowing with goodness or, as the Bible says, with milk and honey, the children of Israel allowed their current circumstances to affect their ability to believe in the good that was to come. Can you imagine a trip that was supposed to take eleven days taking forty years, simply because the travelers did not have the faith to make it through the wilderness any sooner than they did? With faith, the trip would have taken eleven days; but because of doubt, it took them forty years.

As you reach toward your goals, you may have to walk through the wilderness. You may come to a place between pursuing your dreams and actually realizing them that feels like a deserted place. This deserted place tests whether or not we can believe in our dream even when we cannot see it. Faith is, indeed, "the substance of things hoped for, the evidence of things not seen" (Heb. 11:1 NKJ). Even if you cannot see it now, faith will help you see your dream come to fruition in your life. Unlike the Israelites, we must muster up enough faith to hang in there, believing that we will get to the promised land of our dreams.

If there is no struggle, there is not progress.
Those who profess to favor freedom and yet deprecate agitation
are men who want crops without plowing up the ground,
they want rain without thunder and lightening.
They want the ocean without the awful roar of its many waters.
This struggle may be a moral one, or it may be a physical one,
and it may be both moral and physical, but it must be struggle.
Power concedes nothing without a demand.
It never did and it never will.

—Frederick Douglass[2]

Have you ever heard the Bible verse, "Faith without works is dead" (James 2:20)? This says to us that if we are to reach our goals, we must believe in them, but we must also work toward them. You cannot simply pray for a job, but never send out a resume. How is God going to bless you with a job if you don't do your part and send out your resume?! Our vision, dream, and purpose amount to nothing if we do not put in work toward making them happen. You have to water the seed you planted! How will a seed ever grow into what you have planted it to be if you don't water it? Without growth, without movement in a positive direction, you will be just like those Israelites who circled that same ol' tired mountain for forty years.

⊚

You have to leave the city of your comfort
and go into the wilderness of your intuition.
What you'll discover will be wonderful.
What you'll discover is yourself.[3]

—Alan Alda

SEEDS OF DREAMS

I believe that even when we were in our mother's womb, God planted a seed in each of us. This seed holds within it the manifestation of our dreams and our purpose. Along the way, as we grow and move through infancy, childhood, adolescence, and into adulthood, our seeds are either watered with positive, nurturing water that helps the seed God planted into us to grow or not. If the seed is not nurtured, weeds begin to grow, hindering the growth of our dream, purpose, and destiny. These weeds also hinder our growth, self-esteem, self-worth, vision, and ultimately our future. While we cannot change how our seeds were tended to in the past, from this day forward we can choose to water the seed or allow the negative weeds to continue to grow. We can choose to uproot every negative weed of our past by speaking positive words, having positive people in our lives *(we'll talk about this in the next chapter),* thinking positive thoughts, and whatever else is required to make our seed grow. It is up to us to choose positive seed growth, actions, and thoughts or to allow those negative weeds to continue to fester, just like the Israelites did. What will you choose?

If we choose to allow our seeds to grow, we must focus on that one thing that will allow us to continue to believe in spite of what we may or may not see. We must find that one vision or symbol of our vision that we can hold onto until we reach our goal. This is how we keep our eyes on the prize. That is why I encouraged you to write your vision so that it can be your continued focus. In an earlier chapter we discussed a few examples of women who did not allow situations and circumstances to get in the way of believing that they could reach their goal, their promised land. Let's revisit these sisters.

Tyra Banks, as you will recall, struggled to make it in the fashion industry because of her race. But she believed in her dream, kept her eyes on the prize, and not only became a successful fashion model, but an actress, television talk show host, and producer. Tyra exemplifies the importance of believing in your dreams and not allowing roadblocks to stop you from reaching your goal! Even when people stand in your way, Tyra shows us that you can hold your head up high and not quit!

Remember Vanessa Williams, the first African American Miss America? Halfway through her reign she was forced to resign after the release of pornographic photos she had appeared in years earlier. Yet, Vanessa did not let her past stop her. She dreamed of becoming an actress, singer, and Broadway performer. Today, she continues to live out that vision and has succeeded because she believed she could make it and did not look back! Vanessa exemplifies the importance of believing that you can achieve your goals in spite of your past. She shows us that if you focus on moving forward instead of looking back, you can make it!

Finally, you know Beyonce Knowles as one of the most successful R & B artists of our time. However, you may not remember that she struggled after the two original members of Destiny's Child left the group, causing controversy and rumors to fly. Yet unlike some groups that never make it beyond such scandals, Beyonce was able to regroup (literally and figuratively). Beyonce did not allow anyone to deter her from reaching her goal. Beyonce shows us that even when people on your team leave you or betray you, you should never give up on your dream. Like Beyonce, if you keep your eyes on the prize, you can realize your dreams!

Tyra, Vanessa, and Beyonce are not the only women who became successful by believing in their dreams. There are many others like them: Oprah Winfrey, Marva Collins, Harriet Tubman, Rosa Parks, Coretta Scott King, Madame C. J. Walker, and a host of many other women, who achieved because they believed. What was it that allowed them to believe? What allowed them to have enough faith to stay in the fight even when everything around them discouraged them from believing in their dreams? They did not allow their wilderness experience to become their focus. Instead, they continued to believe that their God-given gifts and faith would allow them to reach their goals. If they can do it, so can you! You must have faith in God and belief in yourself to stay in the game, to water the seed that God has planted in your heart. If you can take the time to learn the lessons in the wilderness, if you stay positive, keep the faith, and focus on your dream, you can move into your promised land. The choice is yours; you can choose to live in fear or by faith.

There is yet another example of a woman who lived in faith, when she could have easily and justifiably taken the route of fear. That woman is Mary, the mother of Jesus. Imagine being an unmarried teenager made pregnant by the Holy Spirit. Can you imagine telling your girlfriends that you got pregnant by God!? Not only are you pregnant by God but you are carrying God's son? Can you imagine the number of haters that talked about her, laughed at her, thought she was crazy? Can you imagine how afraid Mary must have been? Yet she pressed on for nine long months, in spite of her fears.

So whenever you think about pressing forward in spite of your fear, think about Mary. Believe that God has uniquely gifted you to do what God has called you to do. It may not be as monumental as giving birth to the Savior, but like Mary, God has given you what you need to do what God has called you to do. So believe in the dream God has placed in your heart. Do not let fears of circumstances, others' judgment, or anything else deter you from living your life's purpose. Keep moving, even when you are afraid.

Now, as I said before, this is what you call seed-time and harvest. What do you think farmers do when they first plant a seed? They come back and water it *every day* and sometimes twice a day. They water a ground that has no trace of anything coming up from it. They go back day after day pouring water on that lifeless dirt, and do you know why? Because they believe something will grow even when they see *nothing* there. This is what keeps them coming back to water day after day; it is their belief, their faith that brings them back out to the crop day after day to water the seeds they have planted, pulling up weeds as they come and taking care of the soil, which will fertilize their seed.

The point is, if you believe it will come up out of that ground and you continue to water it, even when you cannot see anything happening, then one day all of that watering will result in that seed sprouting up out of the ground into a beautiful flower of your dream that is manifest in your life. However, if over time you begin to doubt that the watering is working and stop watering it all together, of course it will *never* grow. This is the same thing we must think of when it comes to our dream, our passion, our purpose. It may take many years of watering before we see anything, but the point is, we can receive, if we believe. *We must have faith!*

Look at Beyonce . . . she believed.

Look at Oprah . . . she believed.

Look at Tyra Banks . . . she believed.

Look at Marva Collins . . . she believed.

Look at Rosa Parks . . . she believed.

Look at Harriet Tubman . . . she believed.

Look at Coretta Scott King . . . she believed.

Look at Madame C. J. Walker . . . she believed.

Look at Halle Berry . . . she believed.

Look at Michelle Obama . . . she believed.

I could go on and on. The point is, these women are not the first to have a dream, to have a vision, a purpose designed for their lives that they had to work toward. What makes these women different from most is that they believed long enough to see it into fruition. They did not give up on watering their seed before it began to grow. They kept the water coming, and look at the beautiful flowers their lives have become.

This all comes down to the popular saying "believe and receive or doubt and do without," and what will you do?

What will you choose?

Will you be emancipated or incarcerated?

Faithful or fearful?

Fear is the reluctance to move forward, but faith says, "I can do all things through Christ who strengthens me" (Phil. 4:13 NKJ).

Will you be chained or free?

Chained by your past or the definition others have placed on you, or free to be exactly who you dream to be?

Defeated or a conqueror?

Issues cause you to feel defeated; faith says, "We are more than conquerors" (Rom. 8:37).

Say with me: My struggles do not define me, my yesterdays do not hold me, my haters do not mold me. The past is dead . . . and tomorrow is the light on my path.

You must promise yourself that never again will you allow negative people, places, and things to define your future. You must move forward without doubt, planning your work and working your plan. You must now vow to keep the promises you have made to yourself.

I will close this chapter with a poem shared with me by one of my closest friends, Dr. Teri Rhetta, as something she used to keep her motivated as she was going through her medical residency. It has become one of the poems that I live by and I hope that it inspires you to keep moving in the direction of your dream. I recommend that you read this poem any time you feel as though you need a little extra nudge in faith's direction. Read this poem whenever you feel as though you can't make it. Anytime you start to look at yourself through the glasses of your past. And, whenever you read this poem, please know that I am right there with you, reading it, too! As we read it, it will help us each to blossom into the beautiful flowers we are capable of becoming. Collectively, we will become a beautiful garden, shining and on display for God's great pleasure!

THE OPTIMIST CREED[4]

Promise yourself

To be so strong that nothing can disturb
your peace of mind;

To talk health, happiness, and prosperity
to every person you meet.

To make all your friends feel that there is
something special [worthwhile] in them.

To look at the sunny side of everything
and make your optimism come true.

To think only of the best, to work only
for the best, and expect only the best.

To be just as enthusiastic about the successes
of others as you are about your own.

To forget the mistakes of the past and press
on to the greater achievements of the future.

To wear a cheerful countenance at all times
and give every living creature you meet a smile.

To give so much time to the improvement
of yourself that you have no time to criticize others.

To be too large for worry, too noble for anger,
too strong for fear, and too happy to permit
the presence of trouble.

—Christian D. Larson

⊠   ⊠   ⊠

DEFINING QUESTIONS

1. What will you choose? Will you believe and receive or doubt and do without?

2. If you choose to believe, what can help you continuously increase your faith on your journey?

The **I** of Define

INVESTMENT

· 6 ·

WHO IS ON YOUR TEAM?

Since the beginning of the book, our focus has been on you. In this chapter, we will focus on who is around you. Who is on your team? In whom are you investing your time and energy, and who is investing their time and energy in you? The people around you can have a profound impact on your life. So it's important that you choose the right core group of friends or team members. The best way to understand the meaning of your core is through the example of an apple.

An apple core has not just one seed, but a group of seeds. The core group of seeds in the apple are watered, given plenty of sunlight, and nurtured, one to the other, so that they all grow collectively, until the core group of seeds becomes an apple. If one seed does not get fertilized, it does not grow. What does that mean for the other seeds? They do not grow either. If just one of those seeds is rotten, then the apple is rotten to the core. Whatever happens to one member of this core group of seeds happens to all the rest.

The same applies to your core. Who are your friends? Who is on your team? The group of people closest to you influences how you feel about yourself, how you dress, where you go, your outlook on your future, even how hard you work toward your goals! A hardworking friend might inspire you to keep challenging yourself and to keep working toward your goals. But a negative friend might try to convince you that you are wasting your time or that you are not capable of achieving your goal. Think about who is currently in your core. Then ask yourself what kind of friends you have working on your team. Who is making up your core?

Only you can choose your team. You can choose team members who will hinder your dream, passion, and excitement and keep you from achieving. Or you can choose people who are uplifting and positive and push you to grow and do better. The choice is yours.

*As iron sharpens iron, so a [wo]man
sharpens the countenance of her friend.*

—Prov. 27:17 (NKJ)

You must find a team that will pull you into your strongest self rather than choosing one that will hold you back from being your best! You must pick a team that will help you win. After all, what is the point of having a team if you are not playing to win?

HERE'S THE LINEUP

Let's look at the players on your team. Every game needs a group of players who fulfill a specific role. When you pull from a team's talents collectively and they are all playing at their best, the team has a greater possibility of winning the game. Just as it is necessary for sports teams to have the right combination of players, it is equally important in this game of life for us to have the right team. In order to have the combination of team members to win the game, the members of your team should consist of the following players: mentors, motivators, counselors, confronters, cheerleaders, and "sista girls." As we begin to look at each of the members of your team—the players—to be in the moment, we will further explore the team concept using the game of basketball. Basketball is a team sport in which the goal is to score points. Scoring points is like working toward reaching goals, moving in a positive direction, and living life to the fullest. Defeat can be equated to losing points, moving negatively in life, never setting or reaching goals, never doing better, and always settling for less than the best. To lose is to be happy with being stuck not working toward any goals or a better life for you.

Let's look at the members of your team who help you become a winner!

Mentors

Every woman needs someone in her life who has already been where she's trying to go. A mentor is a more experienced person who can guide you toward your goal. She is a teacher, a role model, and a counselor who can point you in the right direction. She is someone who has worked hard to get where she is and can inspire you to do the same. She is a trusted guide who can help you find your way when you don't know quite what to do to get where you are going. Her role on a basketball team is the coach. The coach works on plays with you but will not actually play the game for you. Instead, she sits on the sidelines watching you play and giving you the encouragement you need to play well. In between quarters, she can help you strategize your next move, so you can always make the best possible effort. Her goal is to help you come up with the plays that will help you score enough points to meet life goals.

Motivator

Second, every woman needs someone who will push her to step up her game or to get in the game all together. A motivator is someone who consistently encourages you to work toward your dream and who helps keep you excited and on target. She is positive and does whatever it takes to move you to action. This is someone who wants success for you as much as you want if for yourself. Her role on a basketball team is point guard. The point guard organizes the team's offense by making sure that the ball gets to the right player at the right time. In order to truly motivate you, she must have an instinctive knowledge of the game. She must be a good dream holder (in basketball terms this would be a good ball handler) and a great passer, who passes along new ideas or people. She must be quick on her feet and able to play good hard-nosed defense, so that you will not be deterred from your dream! Above all, her ego must not be so inflated that it interferes with her judgment. She must be just as excited about your dream as you are and not become envious when you are making things happen. Your point guard continues to keep you motivated, every step of the way.

Counselor

A woman also needs someone who will listen. This person is someone who will not allow you to wallow in the negative and who will help brainstorm ways to get you out of negative thoughts and circumstances. She is someone who can offer advice, opinions, or instructions and help find solutions to any problem or issue. This person will not judge you, but will encourage you or just listen when you need a empathetic ear. She will process things with you, help you weigh your options in order to make the best choice. Her role on a basketball team is power forward. The power forward plays offensively, listening and helping to sort through where you are on the way to where you are going. She must be a solid rebounder, both offensively and defensively. Like the center, she must be a good passer and a good scorer. She must help you stand up to the opposition at both ends of the court.

Confronter

Next, every woman needs a friend who will tell her the truth, someone who will call her on the carpet and tell it like it is. A confronter is someone who will analyze and evaluate your behavior and tell you about it in a way to help you improve. The trick to this kind of friend is that you must be willing to accept her criticism, so that you can improve and develop. However, her criticism must come from a loving place. Her goal must be to build up, not tear down. Her role on a basketball team is center. She must be an aggressive rebounder and lead the way to show you areas of your life that need improvement. She must prove by her manner and actions that she knows what she is talking about. She must be a dependable scorer and good passer and be able to view the court that the game is played on at all times. That way she can give the most critical and needed advice. She must be strong, resilient, loyal, and trustworthy.

Cheerleader

Every team needs a great cheerleader. This is someone who makes you feel good about who you are and where you are. She is uncritical, enthusiastic and supportive. She offers affirming words and believes in you, even when you do not believe in yourself. Like any cheerleader, she encourages you to stay in the game and not to give up regardless of the cost. She says things like, "You can do it!" and "Dribble . . . shoot, shoot . . . take that ball to the hoop, hoop." We all need a little cheerleading in our lives to bring out the sun on those cloudy days. She is the one who can find the positive in the negative and can give just enough hope to keep you from giving up. Her encouragement gives the boost you need to stay in the game.

Sista Friends

Everyone needs that one special girlfriend that you can just hang with. This is the friend who makes you laugh and takes your mind off stress, if only for a moment. This is the woman in your life who is a lot of FUN! She is someone with whom you can unwind. She is someone who makes taking a break fun and also helps keep you focused on your dreams, even during the downtime. Her role on a basketball team is the small forward. The small forward must be quick, fast, and an adequate rebounder who can lift up your mood in a moment's notice. She must be able to play this type of defense from anywhere on the floor. Most of all, she must be a good scorer. Her points go into the happy basket. Having fun and putting a smile on your face are her most important objectives.

Ladies, those are the players who make up a winning team. Now take note that some members of your team may fit into more than one category, and that is totally fine. The key to having a great team is to make sure you have someone who functions in each of these roles.

Your Mate

There is one more member of your team whom we have not mentioned, and that is your mate. You must choose a mate who believes in you, loves you unconditionally, and supports your dream. His role on a basketball team is the sixth man. The sixth man is the player who can set aside ego and sit on the bench, but be prepared to come off the bench at a moment's notice. When called off the bench, he is able to jump right in the game and do what needs to be done to win. Sometimes he scores, plays exceptional defense, adds rebounding strength; but basically, he does whatever is needed in the game. More than anything else, he gives his team quality minutes when he plays. In order to utilize your sixth man effectively, you must know his capabilities and limitations and allow him a bird's eye view of the game at all times. After all, how can he play at his best if you do not allow him to see what has been happening in the game? Since he doesn't start the game, the sixth man must be given the opportunity to study the game and prepare himself mentally so he is able to get into the flow the moment he steps on the floor.

Having a mate is a blessing, a bonus, though not every winning team has to have one. In fact, the game needs to be played effectively without him before the sixth man can effectively enter. Basketball, as you probably know, is a five-person game. That's why your mate is the sixth man. So before we choose to have a mate in our lives, we must first be happy in life with ourselves and also love who we are prior to having the sixth man enter the game. You must love yourself first; no one can love you for you. At the end of the day, if you cannot play the game without your mate, you definitely will not be able to play the game with him. So develop your skills as player, before you even think about bringing a sixth man off the bench.

QUALITIES OF THE SIXTH MAN

Let's talk a little more intensely about some necessary qualities for your sixth man. The man in your life, the mate that becomes part of your team, must share your mission and goal in life. When you choose a mate, you must choose wisely.

⊕

Therefore shall a man leave his father
and his mother, and shall cleave unto his wife:
and they shall be one flesh.

—Genesis 2:24 (KJV)

I have heard many preachers call this "leave to cleave." So if you are leaving your family to start you own family, it is critical that we take into account to whom we are cleaving. The word "cleave," according to Webster's Dictionary, means to adhere closely; stick; cling; or remain faithful. Sometimes I wonder if we really take the time to think about what it means to cleave when picking our mate. For if we pick a mate based on looks or income, what happens when those things go? What happens when problems arise, when one of you loses a job, when you can't pay your bills, or when you need support to start your dream? What happens as your body ages, you get sick, or you find out you have a life-threatening disease? The mate you choose must be someone willing to stick by you for better or worse, richer and poorer. You must be willing to do the same for him.

I advise that you select your mate based on what I call partnership principles. Choose someone who has been there for you and who you have been there for. Choose someone who has been and will be your friend and partner through it all! There are four ingredients necessary to selecting a mate based on the partnership principles: (1) love, honor, and respect; (2) commitment; (3) celebrating likeness and appreciating differences; and (4) three lives.

Love, Honor, and Respect

Love has no awareness of merit or demerit;
it has no scale. . . . Love loves; this is its nature.

—Howard Thurman

97

What is love? According to the New Living Translation of the Bible:

◎

> *Love is patient and kind. Love is not jealous or boastful*
> *or proud or rude. Love does not demand its own way.*
> *Love is not irritable, and it keeps no record of when it has*
> *been wronged. It is never glad about injustice but rejoices*
> *whenever the truth wins out. Love never gives up,*
> *never loses faith, is always hopeful, and endures*
> *through every circumstance.*
> —(1 Cor. 13:4–7)

Love is not simply a feeling; it is a choice. It is something you must decide to do and to give every day. You must show love in the way that you act and react to one another. When you love someone you are making a commitment to being there through thick and thin, to not love by condition, but to love despite the condition. Love starts with us. In order to love our mates, we must first love ourselves. We must be able to commit to being who we are and what we are. We must love ourselves even when we are still working on ourselves. We must love our imperfections as much as our strengths. We cannot look for someone to love us for us. And we should not choose a mate who does not love us or himself.

Honor and respect go hand in hand with love. So, in this same vein, we must add honor and respect. According to Drs. Gary and Greg Smalley, "Honor simply means deciding to place high value and worth on another person by viewing them as a priceless gift and granting them a position in our lives worthy of great respect."[1] Romans 12:10 (NIV) says, "Be devoted to one another in brotherly love. Honor one another above yourselves." In other words, "Honor is a gift we give to others. It isn't purchased by actions or contingent on our emotions. It may carry strong emotional feelings, but it doesn't depend on them. Rather, it's a decision we make daily toward someone who is special and valuable to us."[2]

Relationships are made up of two different people who become a union, merged together out of feelings of deep affection, high respect for self-worth, and esteem for one another. These ingredients make up love, honor, and respect. You must love, honor, and respect what you both bring to the relationship. Love, honor, and respect means you walk beside your mate, not behind him. These values define your relationships, not superficial material things like who has the most money, the biggest car, and the fanciest "bling bling." The outside world leads us to believe that a woman should seek a man who can buy her extravagant material things. In addition, negative images from the outside world lead many men to make quick money hustling or selling drugs, so they can buy their mates things. This has directed many men down the wrong path. The outside world also makes some men feel powerful based on the number of babies they produce. The bigger "playa, playa" he is, the more power and prestige he feels. The pursuit of material possessions and the false sense of power lead to the demise of love, honor, and respect in relationships.

True power in a relationship lies in the ability to be committed to the partnership and to make a life together filled with love, friendship, honor, and respect. It lies in working through disagreements using the art of negotiation. It lies in loving your mate enough to hang in there together through the rough patches. True power lies in respecting who each of you is and what you bring to the table. This is easy to do when there is money in the bank, but what happens when the record deal or NBA contract goes sour and your mate goes from superstar to unemployed? What happens when there is not money in the bank and the lights in your house are going to be shut off? The true test of love, honor, and respect is when things are going wrong. Do you respect each other enough to hang in there through the rough patches? Does your mate respect you enough to do the same for you? Are you willing to roll up your sleeves when times get tough? Are you willing to get off that bench and play the game? Or, are you only committed to the material possessions you have, and you're ready to bounce when those things are gone?

*Love is more than three words
mumbled before bedtime.*
*Love is sustained by action, a pattern of devotion
in the things we do for each other every day.*

—Nicholas Sparks

In a partnership, love, honor, and respect do not come out of material pursuits but from a true commitment.

Commitment

*Individual commitment to a group effort—
that is what makes a team work, a company work,
a society work, a civilization work."*[3]

—Vince Lombardi

Commitment is the true cornerstone to any partnership. Commitment, according to Webster's dictionary, is the act of committing to a charge, it is an agreement or a pledge, it is the state or an instance of being obligated or emotionally impelled. Let's look at commitment, once again, using the team concept.

If you have ever been part of a winning team, then you have seen what cooperation looks like. Cooperation is created through the synergism of each individual's effort combining to create a group effort. When all members are playing the game at their best, they are committed not only to winning the game, but to their teammates and the role that they have on the team. It is the team's combined efforts that are greater than the sum of each individual's efforts. Similarly, when a couple makes a commitment, they become a team and they join together to make a new branch on the family tree. While they still are a part of their own families, they have left their respective families to make their own life together. No matter what team you played on before, once you have committed to your spouse, you must be fully committed to playing on the same team. Now how can you be on the Lakers and in your heart you are still playing for the Celtics? You may have been on the Celtics; you may have been drafted by the Celtics right out of high school. However, now you play with the Lakers and while the Celtics might have helped you grow and learn, you now must use all you have become to be a true, committed Laker. You may not always agree with the Lakers plays, but at the end of the day you must learn to be able to agree to disagree and do what is best for the team. It is letting go of self and committing to do what is needed to win the game. How does this translate to family? Well you can disagree, but in a partnership you must be able to agree to disagree. What this means is when you do not agree you must be willing to ultimately do what is best for each other and the family, whether you agree with it or not. That is commitment at its highest degree. After all, being in a relationship is not all about the individual, but about the team as a whole. Remember that the letter "I" does not appear in the word "team."

Another important part of commitment is the art of forgiveness. Just as you agree to disagree, you must also be willing to forgive your mate when he makes mistakes. After all, *your relationship is a blending of two imperfect people living in an imperfect world*. If you are not perfect, why do you expect your mate to be perfect? We all have flaws and we all make mistakes. If we expect our mate to put up with and accept our mistakes, we must accept and forgive our mate's mistakes as well. As author Peter Griffiths puts it, "Both of you have to work actively at forgiving the behavior of the other, and forgiving yourself as well, for your own mistakes. That is a tough part of a commitment, for when you feel hurt, it is not that easy to forgive."[4] This is in essence what some would call unconditional love. Unconditional love, according to author Kathy Brandt, is a term that means "loving without limitations, conditions, or reservations."[5] In conditional love, love is earned by a set of conditions; however, unconditional means that I love you as you are, faults and all. So if you are making a commitment to someone, it is not based on conditions or what you can buy me, it means that we are partners and I hold your hand in whatever battle that we face. It means that I trust you, I respect you, and I appreciate who you are. It means we are honest, sincere with, and loyal to one another. However, it is important that both of you come to this relationship, partnership, or marriage with this agreed upon; if just one of you is feeling this way, it will not work. If unconditional love is to work in a relationship, both parties must be fully committed to practicing it.

Now just as there must be unconditional love in commitment, and you must agree to disagree and to forgive, it is also important that you celebrate your likenesses and appreciate your differences.

Celebrating Likeness and Appreciating Differences

In any partnership, you will find some aspects that you have in common and some you do not. Celebrating likeness and appreciating differences can make for a wonderful partnership that will endure through time. It is important for you and your mate to have a similar outlook or purpose, to be of the same mind and spirit about certain issues. These issues include child-rearing, how finances will be handled, religious values, and how you will plan for retirement. In fact, these factors should be considered when you are dating, and these concepts should be factored into the equation of your decision of becoming life partners. Selecting according to these important factors can determine whether your life together will be a great friendship and partnership or a disaster. Let's look at it from a corporate perspective.

If you were starting a company and you wanted to find someone to run it with you, wouldn't you look for someone who thinks like you and with whom you agree with about the direction of the company? If you went into business with someone with whom you do not share the same values and goals for the company, it would be difficult for the company to flourish. Even if you and your mate don't always agree on every detail, it is important that that you agree on the basics and that you determine these issues by having important conversations before marriage. Waiting until you are married to find out that you have absolutely nothing in common and that you disagree on essential issues with your spouse is way too late.

◎

> *Do not be unequally yoked together with*
> *unbelievers. For what fellowship has*
> *righteousness with lawlessness? And what*
> *communion has light with darkness? . . . Or what*
> *part has a believer with an unbeliever? And what*
> *agreement has the temple of God with idols?*
> —2 Cor. 6:14–16a (NKJ)

These powerful Bible verses definitely speak to faith, but I believe also speak to the totality of the partnership you create. If you look deeper into these verses they also speak to being like-minded. Your mate should be someone who is on the same page as you are and someone with whom you see eye to eye. For you want to look for someone who, as I heard Bishop T. D. Jakes say on his show one Sunday morning, "knows what's in your heart before you even say it because it is in his heart, too."[6]

Being in partnership also means that this is someone who will love more than just your body but someone who can love your mind, your heart, and your soul. He is a man who loves every part of you and he gets to experience every part of you. After all, if he only knows one part of you, how can you determine if you are on the same page overall? The man in your life can only operate based on the part of you he knows. So if he does not get to know all of you, he cannot form a true partnership with you. I am astounded by the number of women with whom I have worked in life coaching sessions or with whom I have spoken after one of my workshops who admit to holding part of themselves back in their relationship. It amazes me the number of couples who get married without their mates knowing all about them. Truth be told, it took me so long to find my partner because I wanted to find someone who truly understands the spiritual, intellectual, silly, multiple-projects-going, Imani-mission-focused woman that I am. I am thankful that I waited, because it is hard to fully enjoy your relationship if you cannot allow your mate to see all of what and who you are or be all of who you are for that matter. Your relationship can only truly flourish if both you and your mate fully open up every part of yourselves to each other.

Now just as we are like-minded in some areas, there will also be areas that you will find difference. Areas of difference are usually where disagreements, conflicts, or misunderstandings will occur. In these times of discord, the art of negotiation is a vital tool. Neither of you should try to have the last word nor should you yell at each other. Rather, each of you should talk to each other and try to appreciate one another's perspective on the matter, even if it becomes uncomfortable. You must talk thoroughly about the matter until it is settled or a compromise is reached. Remember, to compromise means that you will not get everything you want. This is a place where you must let go of ego. It means that you will need to be willing to do what is the best for the team, even if it means that you do not get your way. Some disagreements arise when each partner does not understand and appreciate the different roles we play in the partnership. After all, a partnership requires different roles for different people. In some relationships, the woman makes dinner; in others the man does. In some relationships, the woman becomes a stay-at-home mom; in others the man is the stay-at-home dad. In still others, the woman is the primary breadwinner; in others, the man is. You must define the roles in your relationship in a way that works best for you and your mate, and not base it on what everyone else thinks you should be doing.

My husband and I call the roles we play in our marriage our gigs. He has his gigs and I have mine. Once we have established who has which gig, we can say to each other, "Honey, I need you to do your gig." It may be as simple as taking out the trash. Yes, I can do it, but if I constantly do his gig by taking out the trash, over time he will think I don't trust him enough to do his gig. However, if I remain patient enough for him to do his gig, he will do it in his own time and will still feel like he has his role. Letting our mate fulfill his role is the hardest thing for some of us to do. It is hard because we want things done our way in our time. However, we have to understand that the mate in our life is his own person and may not operate within our time frame. Trust that he will do his part. Don't get all in his face, rolling your neck and telling him how trifling he is. If he has not been pulling his weight, then more than likely he wasn't pulling his weight before you decided to get into a serious relationship with him. The issue here is yours: why did you decide to accept this in the beginning but will not accept it now? However, if not pulling his weight is something that seems new, maybe he is going through a rough patch and needs you to be patient and understanding for the moment. Nagging or bugging him does not make the situation better, just trust that he will get back to doing his gig when has had the space to handle his concern. Continue to love, honor, and respect him and remain committed to the team. Remember who your mate is and respect the time and space he may be in. Be a partner, a team member; don't give the ball away to the other team. You can do it if you are willing to stick in there and play to win.

Three Lives

The final partnership principle I will share with you is the principle of three lives. Often when we become life partners we lose self. We lose our own interest and hobbies. We lose our projects and the things we may like to do alone with our girlfriends or in our spare time. Instead, our mate becomes the center of our world. In time, we begin to feel lifeless, resenting our mate for taking this from us, even though he did not take it at all, we freely gave it. We gave it up to him when we lost our own life in creating one with him. Being independent has been many a black woman's strength. We must not lose this when we become joined with our mate. This is what I call having three lives.

I must credit my husband for coming up with the "three lives" principle. I had the benefit of dating a man whose first marriage did not work out and who was determined that his second one would. He came up with this term of us having to have three lives: his, mine, and ours together. This powerful concept is very important in order to create a happy home. You cannot depend on anyone else to make you completely happy. If you think you are getting married so your mate can make you happy, make you complete, and become your whole life, you are in for a rude awakening. You must bring your whole self to the marriage, as must your spouse. Then together you can develop the partnership principle of having three lives. You have your girlfriend outings; he has his guy nights out. You have your ladies lunch; he has his fellas card games; he has his brotherhood meetings and you have your sisterhood mall visits. But together you have a life full of love and commitment that no time and space apart can take away. Because you have your own life outside of his, you each bring your whole rich lives to the table to create one life, a full and rich life that includes him, you, and the two of you. Please don't get the message that having some part of your life separate means it is OK to have a secret life. Don't think these other lives involve cheating on one another or anything of the like. It does mean continuing to be involved in your own hobbies and interests that may not be of interest to your mate. That way, when you have your time together; you are updating each other on your extracurricular activities. Your time together will be that much more special if you can talk about different things that each of you has done.

OTHERS AT THE GAME

Now that you know what players should make up your team, it is time to understand the role of others who are at the game. They are those watching the game (the audience) and those on the opposing team.

The Audience

Those in the audience are usually people who do not mean us any harm, but who do not need to be on our team because their lives are so messy. We have to be careful that the messiness of their lives does not affect our team's ability to win. They may not be bad people, but they come with a lot of drama. I am in no way saying to close the door to those friends who are in your audience, but it may be that they may not be capable of being on your team or in your inner circle at this moment. That may change at some point in the future, but if it is the case that this person would not make a good team member at the moment, you must be unapologetic about ensuring they stay seated in the audience. After all, if this person's issues are overtaking her life, she just may not be at the capacity yet to be on your team because of this. The difference with these folks is that they are trying to do better, they just aren't there yet. So be the kind of friend that you would want as well. You can be the light at the end of the tunnel, telling your friends in the audience to stop being so negative. Be careful, however, that your effort to help them through their situations does not take you out of your own game by sucking you into their drama.

The Opposing Team

Next we turn to the opposing team. This is the group of folks who turn their backs on you when you need them the most, or when your back is turned stab you in it. These people are often jealous of you and feel hatred towards you. I like to call these folk drinkers of the "hateration Kool-Aid." These are the people who talk about you behind your back and put out messages that create negative images and thoughts about you to others. If you allow them to, they can create destruction in your life. These are the people who have disappointed you, said something or done something to intentionally hurt or anger you. Their negative behaviors make it difficult for you to maintain trust in the relationship.

Just being around negativity keeps negative energy around you, and it can keep you from pursuing your dream. When you continue to argue over what they have done or even think about it over and over, it just makes you more upset or hurt. It gives energy to it that you could redirect to something much more positive. In fact, the negative emotional space this relationship puts you in takes your joy. You wind up giving people like this the remote control to your life. Yes, you allow them to push your buttons just like you push the buttons on a remote control to get the television to do what you want it to do. You must stop giving people your remote so they can access and push your buttons. You give your remote to anyone or anything you allow to control how you feel. This negativity can consume you if you decide to stay in it. What do you do when friends have gone from playing on your team to playing on the opposing team? When they have your remote and are taking what could be a positive situation and making it negative? You must let them go!

LETTING PEOPLE GO!

Someone may have started out on your team but, over time, situations and circumstances have placed them on the opposing team. Having someone who was once on your team join the opposing team can be difficult. In order to keep yourself in the positive, working toward your goal, you must keep a positive and/or healthy mind, body, and spirit. In order to keep yourself in this positive space, you must get rid of all negative people, emotions, and thoughts that take up your space and steal your joy. Negative people can infiltrate your entire being and affect your self-esteem and self-image. As difficult as it may be to part with certain people who may have even been in your life for a long time, you must let go!

Letting go means to release and to forgive anyone or anything that has hurt you or offended you. By forgiving, releasing, and letting go, you are by no means acting like your feelings of hurt, anger, and/or hatred do not exist. There is no way to get rid of the circumstances that have made you feel the way you do. However, by letting go you are choosing to no longer allow the circumstances to negatively affect you. You are letting go of what these feelings do to you, avoiding staying stuck and dwelling on those feelings and the circumstances that cause them. You are accepting what has happened and moving on from it. Instead of remaining focused on yesterday, you set your sights on tomorrow.

To do this you have to be determined to move on with your life by cleansing yourself of the negative emotions. By doing this, you take back your remote, your power, and release the hold these negative emotions have had on you. You reclaim your own power and give yourself peace of mind, and you go back to moving in a positive direction. Remember that you are not your past and your past cannot hold you in this place without your permission. Leave your past behind and move on . . . LET IT GO! In chapter three we talked about Beyonce, Vanessa Williams, and Tyra Banks, who each had to let go. They had to let go of the people, places, and things that did not believe in them. They too had to let go, and so do you! The sky is the limit, but in order to reach the sky, you must surround yourself with people who will keep you strong and help you grow. By the same token, you must let go of anyone or anything that is holding you back. You must invest in relationships with the people that can help you win the game! Remember, healthy and supportive relationships are worth the time and energy you put into them. Relationships that are negative are not worth your time or energy or even the space they occupy in your life. Let them go!

So who's holding you back, keeping you down, or making you think you cannot be any better than you used to be? You have got to decide not to allow these people to continue to add stress and negativity to your life. Perhaps you have no problem letting go of a person, but you still hold a grudge. Holding grudges is not really letting go, because if you are holding a grudge it means you are still holding on to feelings from the past. In order to move past this, you must not only let go of the person, you must also let go of anger and hurt. Letting go does not require you to forget or ignore. By all means, you should retain the lessons you have learned from your past relationships. However, you need to release emotional baggage you may be carrying around, so that you are open to and present for new relationships to enter your life.

Members of our opposing team can teach us a lot. Let's consider some of the lessons we can learn from our "haters."

DON'T BE A HATER!

There is no explanation for why some women get jealous and drink the "hateration" Kool-Aid while others lift you up for the goals you have set and the things you are accomplishing. We each have our own unique place in this world and, yes, there is room for everyone's dream to be fulfilled! I must borrow my friend, BeNeca Ward's words on this one as she perfectly said, "Understanding that you are not in a race with anyone else in life helps you to better see and understand your personal obstacle course and makes it a little easier to run. People who are most successful are usually not competing with other people, nor are they using other people's 'common' methods. They rise to the top following the original path that was created for them. Don't stress because someone else is at a different level in life than you. Know that you have to climb your own ladder towards GOD's path."[7] So, if you have people in your life who are mad at you because you are doing better, jealous because you are excelling, or hating because you have a new life goal, stop making this a competition for them. You do not have to compete with them. Stop allowing the crabs to try and pull you back into the barrel, and let them go! Here are two considerations when letting go:

1. "Do not be deceived: Evil company corrupts good character" (1 Cor. 15:33 NKJ). Since this is the case, keeping negative, harmful, depressing, and destructive people in your life will produce negative, harmful, depressing, and destructive results. If you want positive, constructive, affirming, encouraging things to occur in your life, surround yourself with people, places, and things that are positive, constructive, affirming, and encouraging. Remember, negative produces negative, and positive produces positive.

2. I am sure you have heard the saying, "Let go and let God." To let go is an act of surrender to the fact that we actually have no control. We cannot control how people act, nor can we control the decisions they make. Instead of fighting what is, we need to learn to accept and to be at peace with what is. We can only control how we allow what others say or do to affect us and how we interact or react to it. By choosing to have peace and trusting that what is meant to be shall be, we can hold onto a more positive outlook about anything that comes our way. By letting go, we actually allow more positive energy to flow to us instead of trying to force what may not be meant to be.

After you have picked your teammates, determined your audience, and let go of your opponents, the last thing you must do is to determine how to best utilize your team. We must invest in our relationships. Making people feel appreciated is the key to maintaining friendships.

HOW TO UTILIZE YOUR TEAM

The whole purpose of having a team is to utilize team members' gifts in ways that will strengthen you. Asking a teammate for help does not mean you are weak; it means you are smart enough to see the strength of your core and to allow their strength to supersede your weakness. Isn't that what team sports are all about? You have to be willing to share yourself and to be open to receiving contributions that others can make to your life.

While others are helping you, it is important that you give back to them. Author and minister Joel Osteen calls this making a deposit. We all must strive to make positive deposits instead of negative withdrawals, making every effort to make relational deposits into people's lives, encouraging them, building them up and helping them to feel better or do better. If we are making deposits on a constant basis, then we are investing in positive energy to come our way in the future. So when we need a little positive energy, we can take from the reserve we have stored up by making all of our positive deposits. However, if we are making negative withdrawals, then there is no reserve to draw from.[8] Indeed, even if we are not taking from the reserve of a specific friend or team member, God has a way of sending back to you whatever you put out. So if I am kind to a complete stranger, God will always send a positive deposit back to me. Now, that is a deposit I definitely want to continue to invest in.

It is also important to take note of how you treat your team or anyone else with whom you come in contact. If people do something nice for you, help you with something you are working on, support you in any kind of way, it is important to make them feel appreciated for what they have done for you. Take a moment to write a thank-you note, give them a small token of appreciation, invite them over to you home for lunch, or any other act of appreciation. Keep in mind that folks are not obligated to help you or be there for you, so make them feel like you value them as a friend. Make them feel treasured for what they have done for you.

In essence, do unto others . . . "And just as you want people to do to you, you also do to them likewise" (Luke 6:31NKJ). The only way to have a friend is to be one. You should treat others the way you want to be treated.

MIND YOUR MANNERS

As we think about how to treat people, we must also look at manners, as character, taste, etiquette, and conduct all go hand in hand with making sure people feel appreciated and respected. As you define your team as well as yourself, you want to make sure all those you come in contact with feel respected and appreciated. To do so, consider the following definitions according to Webster's dictionary:

> *Manners:* your way of speaking to and treating others. Your way of doing and saying things.

> *Style:* grace or polish in a person's manners or actions; elegance or luxury.

> *Respect:* high admiration or esteem for oneself as well as for a person or quality; polite regard or consideration and the definition of being a lady.

> *Lady:* a woman of good social position, breeding. This breeding is a conscious decision to learn and show good manners in who one is and how one interacts with others.[9]

So, to relate manners with how you treat people, think about how your actions and words make people feel. If you don't want people to disappoint you, don't leave them hanging. If you do not want people to say unkind words to you, don't say unkind words to them. Once we put words out there we cannot take them back. It's not like we can write our words and actions in pencil and then erase them once we realize what we've said or done something mean, hurtful, or disrespectful. With this in mind, it kills me to hear women refer to one another as the "B" word. Is that supposed to be a positive word? Does the word bit__ lift you up and make you feel good about yourself? If it does, why is it used to also tear people down? I can say the same thing about the word "N" word. Why is it OK for our friends to call us "my nigga" but if a white person says "what's up, my nigga" it is not OK? Think about that.

❋

The N-word still has a negative
connotation, which suggests both self-hatred
and the projection of the same hate against other
black people, including the "bit__es" and "hos"
who represent their mothers and sisters.[10]

—Bill Cosby and Alvin Pouissant

Think about the negative messages we are putting out there from just the words we speak to one another. We must use the same standard for everyone; we must treat people as we want to be treated, and remember to mind our manners. I do not want people to call me the B word, whether it is my girlfriends or a enemy, so I do not call anyone that, nor do I allow anyone to call me that. The point is that we must treat others with love and respect if that is what we want to receive in return. We must speak words that build up and not break down. We must choose those actions in relationships that produce positive results and not make negative space between friends.

Another major key to maintaining friendships is to learn to accept people for who they are. We talked about this in an earlier paragraph but I must repeat this here. Realize that we cannot change anyone. If there is something that someone on your team is doing that bothers you or affects you, realize that the only thing you have the power to change in any given relationship or situation is you! You can change how you react to it, how you allow it to affect you. You can even change the person's position on your team or in your life, but you must realize you cannot change that person! Only that person can change him- or herself. What you must do is learn to love that person and learn to live with it or let go! Accept and move on! Don't stay stuck on thinking you can fix a person, fix a certain personality. Put the focus on you and what you can change about you to deal with whatever it may be.

I hope this chapter has helped give you some perspective on what people you need on your team and how to maintain the team once you have chosen it. Remember the people around you can either help or hinder your ability to define your own way. So as you move forward to defining the new you, be sure to surround yourself with positive people who can help keep you on a positive path.

⊠　⊠　⊠

Defining Questions

1. What type of friend are you?

2. Take a moment and think about the friends who are making a positive contribution to your life and those who are not. Those who are not have to go.

3. What friends are the ones that are definitely on your team?

4. How can you enhance your relationships and make people feel appreciated?

The N of Define

NURTURE

7

GET OFF THE BENCH

Now that we have developed the game plan for defining every major area of your life, it is time for you to get off the bench and get in the game. After all, what is the purpose of developing a plan if you aren't going to work the plan? In this chapter, we will help you get your plan working.

Let's start by looking at all of the areas in your life that you have outlined as you read each chapter. No more brainstorming, it's time to actually write the plays and begin to execute them. So, pull together all the goals we have developed as we went through this book. In essence, this section of the book will help you sum up the you you wish to be, the areas of your life you want to work on, and the team members you need to reach your goals. Then you can begin to work toward your plan, dream, and purpose. If you already know your purpose, then use this opportunity to work on setting new goals or reframing the old ones.

Trying is not an option!

It is easy to talk about what we are going to do but some of us actually never begin to do it. The only way we will live the life of our dreams is not only to write the vision but to actually make a plan toward doing it. So it is important that you not skip this important step. If you do, I can assure you that you will stay stuck where you are. If you choose to do it, you don't have to try! All you have to do is DO IT!! This is where you have the ability to choose to either work on the areas we have gone over together in this book or stay stuck right where you are! This is where you can choose to never do anything new or to become all you can be! My guess is that you don't want to stay stuck; otherwise you would not have read to this point of the book.

LET THE GAME BEGIN!

Go back to the section in chapter 2 where you listed your dreams and your purpose. What do you plan to accomplish immediately and within the next five years? Use the space below to list the steps in your action plan for reaching your dreams.

In chapters 3 and 4, you defined a new vision of yourself. What new choices will you make about how you look? What additional education or training do you need to reach the next level in your career? What do you want out of your job or career? What changes do you need to make in the area of finances or any other area(s) in your life? Take a moment to revisit your goals in these areas. Use the space below to flesh out your plan in these areas.

In chapter 5 we explored faith. What will remind you to believe when you get to your wilderness place? In what ways can you work on your ability to believe and receive?

In chapter 6 we explored relationships, the kind of people you need on your team to help you work toward your dream. Think about the people you will need to make up your team. To whom do you need to give tickets to watch the game and whom do you need to let go?

There is one final thing you need to do to seal the deal, to ensure that you are not just placing words on paper—a contract. A contract is an agreement between two or more parties (such as companies or people) where all parties agree to perform some task or action in exchange for something else. When parties enter into a business relationship a signed contract is a legal document signifying their agreement to do what the contract specifies. I am asking you to enter into a contract, not with me or anyone else, but with yourself. In your contract, you will be making a promise to yourself to do what it takes to define your way and become all the woman you were created to be. You will commit to reaching all the goals you have set for yourself. In your contract, you will state exactly what you will do and outline how you will do it. By signing this contract, you are committing to yourself to work on YOU, to define your own way in life! So let's start our plan by committing to actually doing it! Your contract is on the following pages.

◎ *My Contract* ◎

I, _____ ,

                     Your name   *Date*

today commit to begin my pursuit of

_____ .

My dream

What I need to do to get there is

_____

_____

_____

_____ .

In order to pursue my dream and define my own way,
I commit to do the following:

☐ **TAKE OFF MY CAP:** I will NOT focus on what may have limited me in my past. From this day forward, I will focus on my possibilities.

☐ **BEGIN TO WORK TOWARD MY DREAM OF** _____ . I commit to let determination and perseverance be my guides as I work on my dream. Today, I will begin to work my plan as outlined in chapter 2 so that I can live out my dream.

☐ **TRUST GOD!** I will trust God and the process so that I will get to my promised land.

☐ **BELIEVE IN ME!** I believe in the uniquely wonderful person that I am and choose to love who I am on the way to where I am going.

☐ **MATCH MY OUTSIDE WITH MY INSIDE:** I will make sure that my outer image is a reflection of the person I wish for others to encounter when they see me.

☐ **LET GO OF NEGATIVE:** I will remove negative self-talk and negative relationships from my life.

☐ **PURSUE LIFELONG LEARNING.** I commit to continuously educate myself. I commit to experiencing new things and to lifelong growth.

☐ **ASSERT MYSELF.** I will communicate my needs clearly and will not allow anything negative into my path. I will also make it a point to learn about resources, people, and opportunities that can help me reach my goals.

☐ **PULL TOGETHER MY TEAM.** Today, I commit to thanking the positive people in my life and letting them know my plans for my future and how they can help me get there.

☐ **GAIN CONTROL OF MY FINANCES.** I commit to making a budget and using it. I also commit to saving and setting financial goals for my future.

☐ **GET INVOLVED.** I commit to participating in at least one professional club or organization that will help me expand my resources as I build my dream.

☐ **HAVING FUN.** I commit to having fun and meeting new people but I will not let my socializing interfere with working toward my dream.

☐ **GET ENOUGH SLEEP.** I will make every effort to get at least seven to eight hours of sleep every night during the week.

☐ **EXERCISE REGULARLY.** I will exercise at least three times a week for twenty minutes to relieve stress and keep my body fit.

☐ **TAKE TIME TO RELAX.** I will give myself enough down time to help relieve tension and stress and keep me grounded.

☐ **NOT MAKING EXCUSES!** I can do anything I decide to do if I just take the time to organize my life, utilize my team when I need them, and not let any caps or roadblocks deter me from my dream.

(Please feel free to add more items to your contract here.)

I agree to adhere to all of the above. If need help in order to do so, I will reach out to one of my team members for help.

_____

Print name   Signature   Date

To download this form, see the Imani Life Transformations page at www.imani.org.

Once you have read and signed the contract, I suggest that you make a copy of it and post it where you can look at it every day. Allow it to serve as a daily reminder of what you need to do to get off the bench, get in the game, and define your own way.

If you sometimes have a difficult time following through with commitments and need a little extra push, consider giving a copy of your contract to one or more of your team members. You could even hold a monthly girlfriends' dream-building meeting, especially if you and your friends are going through this process together. Use this meeting to share with one another and hold one another accountable as well as provide encouragement and support. You can even have a little fun while you are working your new plan for your life by holding pampering sessions or potluck dinners during your monthly meetings.

Do whatever you need in order to stay on course. The sky is the limit for you to manifest the desires and dreams that are in your heart. So, my sister, get off the bench and get in the game. Whether you do this as a team effort or deicide to fly solo, you can definitely do anything you set your mind.

Where the will is absent, the way will not be found.

—Michael Eric Dyson

It is time, ladies, to attract all that is good and will allow you to manifest in your life all that you deserve, desire, and dream! You can do this! It's time to *get off the bench!!*

⊠　⊠　⊠

DEFINING QUESTIONS

1. Are there any areas that are not on your contract that you need to also commit to?

2. How will you make a conscious effort to stay on track with the commitment you are making to yourself in the areas you have outlined thus far?

The **E** of Define

ESSENCE

· 8 ·

SHINE!

Let your light shone before others, so that they may see
your good works and glorify [God] in heaven.

—Matt. 5:16

At the beginning of this book, we pondered whether we are fulfilling the legacy left by our ancestors. Each chapter has taken us on a journey to define our own way in life and become all that we were created to be. When we live in our purpose, we not only make our ancestors proud, but we please God in heaven as we shine for the whole world to see. For, when we are being the most positive person we can be, have positive people around us, and are moving in a positive direction toward our life's purpose, our *light* is on! The switch is flipped on. Dare I say, *"BLING, BLING!!"*

The woman who has defined herself in a positive way shuts down every stereotype that has been said about black women. She is not a mammy or a maid. She is not a video girl; nor is she the "B" word or a "ho." Rather, she is a woman who is working toward a life that makes her fulfilled, healthy, happy, wealthy, and complete. Yes, she seeks to live in her passion and purpose in everything she does as a daughter, mother, wife, worker, student, volunteer, community leader, or any role she fills.

So as we embark on this journey to live in the new definition we have created for ourselves, we must remember the keys to living in the light of the life we DEFINE:

DISCOVERY

EDIFICATION

FAITH

INVESTMENT

NURTURE

ESSENCE

We must take the journey of DISCOVERY as we explore what caps we are wearing and no longer allow them to hold us back from living in our life purpose. We must discover our vision and our gifts so that we achieve something that will benefit beyond just ourself, extending out to our village. We must be committed to the EDIFICATION of our self both inside and out as we grow financially, mentally, and spiritually and commit to lifelong learning. We must keep our eyes open so that we learn new things and can see the opportunities before us and grab them! We must have

FAITH, "the substance of things hoped for, the evidence of things not seen." If we can believe it, we can achieve it. Never forget that it is up to each of us to keep the light of hope alive inside us. We must INVEST in having positive energy, positive people, and positive life circumstances around us, as this will produces positive outcomes in our lives. Along the way we must constantly pay attention to where we are, who is around us, and if what we are doing or saying is working for or against our dream, our journey, our definition. If it is not, we must reinvest our energy, moving from that negative to positive. In so doing, we must NURTURE our goals and dreams we have designed for ourselves on this journey of self-definition. We should only allow time for activities, friends, and associates that nurture who we are and add value to our lives, eliminating all negative thinking, negative people, and negative situations, that do not nurture the seed of hope and opportunity. Lastly, we must be aware of our ESSENCE, our soul, spirit, our heart.

As we think, we shall be.
As we believe, we shall receive.

It is within our essence that this belief begins and is watered to reach its harvest. All of the areas we have outlined, thus far, allow our essence to shine, or to glow or radiate! For when we have fully defined ourselves that is what we do, shine!

I hate to tell you this, ladies, but the work does not stop here. In order to keep on shining, there may come a time when you must *refine*. So, yes, we *define—shine* and then sometimes *refine*.

According to Webster's dictionary, "refine" means to free from impurities or to improve or perfect. While we are on this road, we must continually reevaluate where we are and how we are progressing so that we can make the necessary adjustments along the way. I like to call this process "burn it up!" For if you think of your life as being like silver, silver is required to be burned in a fire before it can shine. In fact, most precious metals must be refined before they are ready to be sold. Putting the silver through the fire makes it live out the purpose for which silver was made. So it is for you and me. As God, who is our refiner, puts us in the fire, we will come out better as the essence of who God made us is refined. It is the brightness of our essence that will shine through.

⊚

[God] sits as a refiner and purifier of silver.

—Malachi 3:3 (NKJ)

I don't know about you, but I want to shine. So I am willing to sit through the fires of life for the right amount of time and at the right temperature so that I can be refined. I realize that when we are fully living in our life purpose, when we are reflecting positive energy in and through us, that is when others can see God in us. I realize that God will burn up all the negative energy in us and around us, but we have to be willing to sit in the fire long enough for it to be refined. Negative situations or circumstance may come, but we must keep the faith even when we are in the middle of the fire.

You may be going through the fire right now. In fact, there may have been sections in this book that may have burned you up! That means that is a place that needs to be refined! There may be some situations and circumstances that may be hard to let go, but you must burn them up. There also may be some things you are going to have to endure in order to make it to your promised land. However, stay in that fire. Don't complain about it. Trust God and let it burn up, so that you can reach the land of your dreams. Let whatever needs to be refined! You can no longer ignore it. BURN IT UP! Sit in that fire until God can see the essence of who God created you to be.

When you think there is a door you need to go through to make it toward your dream and that door closes, start looking around for the open window or the back door. For when one door closes, another one is sure to open. Even when you have worked very diligently to set goals and make plans, even when you are working your plan right down to the letter, things may not go as you planned. But you must be open and willing to make the changes needed without losing hope. You may not reach your goals when you thought you would or how you thought you would, but you will get there if you do not lose heart.

You may be wondering why I am telling you this at end of the book after you have done all this hard work. Was this all for nothing? Well, sometimes even after we have charted our course toward fulfilling our dreams, God may have a completely different way of getting us to the promised land. This does not mean your dream is not meant to happen, it just means it may not be meant to happen the way you have drawn it out or planned it.

If you were Beyonce you may have thought Destiny's Child was supposed to have four members, but God thought three was enough. If you were Tyra Banks, you may have thought you would be walking the runway forever, but God said, "How about I give you America's Next Top Model." Sometimes plans switch up and you have got to be willing to *refine* your plan along the way. You have to let go of your dreams manifesting in a particular way at a particular time. Even when that happens, you must never let your light go out. Never allow yourself to begin to think negatively or engage in negative self-talk. Instead keep on smiling, keep shining, and know you can always count on your purpose to be fulfilled if you can just stay in the game. You must take pleasure and love who you are on the way to where you are going.

So I ask the question again: How do you want to be remembered? I hope that as we have journeyed together in these pages and you have engaged in the defining work that has been laid out, you now have a clearer picture of the you you are capable of and desire to become. If you need to refine or redefine any areas of your life, I encourage you to reread any sections that you feel need further study. I look forward to hearing just how your dream turns out. I know you will get there. I also believe you have worked all the way to end of the book because you probably believe you can, too!

So, Go on, girl, . . . SHINE!

THIS BOOK IS A PROGRAM OF IMANI LIFE TRANSFORMATIONS

If you enjoyed the journey of reading this book, then you have begun to carve out areas of your life that you can better define. How exciting it is to embark on a journey to be all that you were created to be! We would like to carry this transformative work to your entire village! To do this, we need your help. Tell your sista friends, neighbors, church young adult group, ladies at the beauty shop, sorority sisters, family, sisters, and coworkers—tell anyone you can think of about the book.

If you have a blog or Facebook page, share with your readers/friends about the book and encourage others to join you in the journey of defining your own way. You could buy a set of books and give them as gifts to women in domestic violence shelters, rehabilitation or homeless programs, or any other places where women are rebuilding their lives. Talk about the book on your e-mail lists, forums, or other places you engage people often. Don't make it sound like a commercial, just share with folks how the book affected you and offer people the link to the Imani Life Transformations page at www.Imani.org so that they too can purchase a copy.

The more women who benefit from this book, the better. After all, this is what Imani Life Transformations is all about—helping African American women become the women they were born to be!!

If you would like to stay connected and committed to the work of *Defining Your Own Way*, please join our blog at www .maximziemoment.wordpress.com. New topics are posted weekly and we would love to hear how things are progressing for you.

If you would like to book Nicole to speak at your next women's conference or retreat, see the Imani Life Transformations page at www.imani.org.

NOTES

Chapter 2

1. Sister Souljah, *No Disrespect* (New York: Vintage, 1996).
2. Rick Carson, *Taming Your Gremlin: A Surprisingly Simple Method for Getting Out of Your Own Way* (New York: Harper Collins, 2003), 10.
3. Paul D. Tieger and Barbara Barron-Tieger, *Do What You Are: Discover the Perfect Career for You through the Secrets of Personality Type* (New York: Little Brown, 2007), 5.

Chapter 3

1. "African American Model: Tyra Banks," *Contemporary Black Biography*, Gale Group, vol. 50, 2005, Biography Resource Center, http ://www.goafrican.com/famous-african-american-models/tyra-banks -african-american-model-02/, accessed June 23, 2010.
2. American Experience, PBS, "People & Events: Breaking the Color Line at the Pageant," http://www.pbs.org/wgbh/amex/missamer-ica /peopleevents/e_inclusion.html, accessed on June 23, 2010.
3. Beyonce Knowles, Anthony Dent, and Mathew Knowles, "Survivor," recorded by Destiny's Child on Survivor Columbia Records, 2001.Used by permission of Matthew Knowles, Music World Entertainment.

4. Marilyn French Hubbard, *Sisters Are Cashing In: How Every Woman Can Make Her Financial Dreams Come True* (New York: Berkley, 2000), 7.

5. Rev. Jesse L. Jackson and Jesse L. Jackson Jr., *It's about the Money: How You Can Get out of Debt, Build Wealth and Achieve Your Financial Dreams* (New York: Times Business, 1999).

6. Hubbard, *Sisters are Cashing In*, 53–54.

7. "Money & Investment Guide: 8 Easy Ways to Start Your Own Business, Make More Money, and Be the Boss," *Essence* (February 2008).

8. Profit Sharing/401k Council of America, http://401k.org/, accessed June 23, 2010. The site includes a wealth of information, including tools for determining how much to save.

9. Bill Cosby and Alvin F. Pouissant, quoting Bernard Franklin, *Come on People: On the Path from Victims to Victors* (Nashville: Thomas Nelson, 2007), 159.

10. Wikipedia Foundation, "Health," http://en.wikipedia.org/wiki/Health, accessed March 15, 2008.

11. Makeisha Lee, "Obesity, Lifestyles and African Americans—What Are the Correlations?" http://www.imdiversity.com/Villages/African/family_lifestyle_traditions/bpr_obesity1127.asp, accessed June 23, 2010.

12. Ibid.

13. Centers for Disease Control, "QuickStats: Prevalence of Obesity among Adults . . . ," from *MMWR Weekly,* October 2, 2009, http://www.cdc.gov/mmwr/preview/mmwrhtml/mm5838a6.htm, accessed June 23, 2010.

14. Jeffry A. Jacqmein, MD, "Why Should I Exercise?" (revised 4/16/99), http://jaxmed.com/articles/wellness/exercise.htm, accessed June 23, 2010.

15. Margie Patlak, "How Much Sleep Is Enough?" *Your Guide to Healthy Sleep,* National Institutes of Health, NIH Publication No. 06-5271, November 2005, page 19, http://www.nhlbi.nih.gov/health/public/sleep/healthy_sleep.pdf, accessed June 24, 2010.

16. U.S. Department of Health and Human Services, The National Women's Health Information Center, "Minority Women's Health: African Americans," http://www.4woman.gov/minority/africanamerican/, accessed June 24, 2010.

17. National Women's Health Inflormation Center, "Protecting Your Reproductive System," www.womenshealth.gov/pub/2007daybook /reproductive/2007Daybook_c07_repro.pdf, page 80, accessed June 24, 2010.

18. Found at http://www.malcolm-x.org/quotes.htm, accessed June 24, 2010.

19. Cosby and Poussaint, *Come on People,* 101.

20. Ibid.

21. Barack Obama, "State of the Union Address" (February 24, 2009) http://stateoftheunionaddress.org/2009-barack-obama, accessed June 24, 2010.

22. *The Great Debaters,* directed by Denzel Washington, Metro-Gold-wyn-Mayer, 2007.

23. University of North Texas (2007) Why Go To College http:// www.unt.edu/pais/howtochoose/why.htm, accessed June 24, 2010.

Chapter 4

1. Dr. Joe Rubino, "Definition: Self-Image," 2008, SelfGrowth.com, the Online Self Improvement Encyclopedia, http://www.selfgrowth .com/articles/Definition_Self Image.html, accessed June 24, 2010.

2. Karl Perera, http://www.more-selfesteem.com/selfimage.htm, accessed June 24, 2010.

Chapter 5

1. "The Daily Word by Rev. Run," crushable.com/entertainment /the-daily-word-by-rev-run.

2. Frederick Douglass, "West India Emancipation Speech," August 4, 1857, quoted portion viewable at http://www.africandiasporastudies .com/downloads/syllabus005.pdf, accessed June 24, 2010.

3. Alan Alda, retrieved from http://www.brainyquote.com/quotes /quotes/a/alanalda107654.html accessed June 24, 2010..

4. "The Optimist Creed," http://www.optimist.org/e/visitor/creed .cfm, accessed June 23, 2010, adapted from Christian D. Larson, "The Optimist Creed," 1912 (original version in Science of Mind 71 (June 1998).

Chapter 6

1. Drs. Gary and Greg Smalley, "What Is Honor," 2006, http:// www.smalleyonline.com/articles/p_whatishonor.html, accessed September 15, 2008.

2. Ibid.

3. Vince Lombardi. BrainyQuote.com, Xplore Inc, 2010, http:// www.brainyquote.com/quotes/quotes/v/vincelomba129818.html, accessed June 24, 2010.

4. Peter Griffiths, "What Is Commitment in a Relationship?" column, *Prince Albert Daily Herald & Rural Roots*, July 8, 2001, http://www .lib.sk.ca/Default.aspx?DN=2aa651fe-f26c-4c16-ad05-05707cfddcef, accessed June 24, 2010.

5. Kathy Brandt, "Unconditional Love (starting with you)," http:// www.selfgrowth.com/articles/Brandt1.html, accessed on June 24, 2010.

6. T. D. Jakes, The Potters Touch TDJ Ministries, TD Jakes Enterprises: Dallas, Texas.

7. BeNeca Ward, "Moment of Focus" series, publication pending.

8. Joel Osteen, "Become a Better You" (New York: Free Press, 2007).

9. William McLeod, ed., *Webster's Concise Dictionary of Modern English* (Nashville: Thomas Nelson, 1987).

10. Bill Cosby and Alvin F. Pouissant, *Come on People: On the Path from Victims to Victors* (Nashville: Thomas Nelson, 2007), 145.

RESOURCE LIST
Defining Your Way Tool Kit

The following is a list of websites and other resources that can aid you on your journey to define your own way. (Please note these websites are listed as resource for you and are not necessarily supported by the author of this book.)

Self-Esteem/Self-Image

More Self-Esteem: http://www.more-selfesteem.com/.

National Association for Self Esteem: http://www.self-esteem-nase.org/.

Self Confidence for Women: http://www.selfesteem4women.com/index.php?ad=7.

Fostering a Positive Self Image: http://www.clevelandclinic .org/health/health-info/docs/4000/4021.asp?index=12942.

Hire an Image Consultant: http://www.imageconsultingexcellence.com/.

Career/College Planning

Occupational Outlook Handbook is a source of career information, which will help you find information about various careers: www.bls.gov/oco/home.htm.

Information on college and career planning as well as financial strategies: http://mappingyourfuture.org/.

Dickson, Delijah S. *Freshman 101: A Road Map & Journal to Surviving Your First Year of College,* www.freshman101.net/home.html.

Money

Black Enterprise, Wealth for Life: http://www.blackenterprise.com/wealth/wealth.asp.

Minding your money (NPR): http://www.npr.org/templates/story/story.php?storyId=9348237.

Suze Orman, personal finance expert: http://www.suzeorman.com/.

Personal finance advice (CNN): http://money.cnn.com/pf/.

Budgeting: http://personalfinancebudgeting.net.

Help with your shopping addiction?: http://debtorsanonymous.org/; http://www.shopaholicsanonymous.org/.

Look at your credit report: http://annualcreditreport.com.

Brooke Stephens' Financial Advice That Makes Sense: http://brookestephens.com.

Health

Black Women's Health: http://www.blackwomenshealth.com/2006/index.php.

Health & Wellness (Black Enterprise): http://www.blackenterprise.com/lifestyle/health-wellness/.

Women's Heath Issues: http://womenshealth.about.com/.

Additional Print Resources

Greene, Bob. *The Best Life Diet.* New York: Simon & Schuster, 2006.

LaBelle, Patti, and Laura Randolph Lancaster. *Patti LaBelle's Lite Cuisine.* New York: Gotham Books, 2003.

OTHER BOOKS FROM THE PILGRIM PRESS

BAD GIRLS OF THE BIBLE
The Sequel
BARBARA J. ESSEX
978-0-8298-1824-6/paper/128 pp/$16.00

Several years ago, Essex launched the bestselling Bible study *Bad Girls of the Bible: Exploring Women of Questionable Virtue*. It has become a favorite of teachers and preachers everywhere, with Bible study groups, sermon series, retreat themes, and seminary classes forming across the country to learn from it and the Bible. Now Essex has returned with a command performance focusing on fourteen new stories of biblical women from the Hebrew Bible and New Testament.

BAD GIRLS OF THE BIBLE
Exploring Women of Questionable Virtue
BARBARA J. ESSEX
0-8298-1339-X/paper/114 pages/$16.00

Designed as a fourteen-week study, this resource explores biblical accounts of traditionally misunderstood or despised women as they are presented in the Bible. Reflection questions are included as well as suggestions for preaching and teaching.

PUT ON YOUR CROWN
The Black Woman's Guide to Living Single ... and Christian
SHERON C. PATTERSON
978-0-8298-1696-9/paper/224 pp/$19.00

Put on Your Crown is a result of the relationship advice Patterson has shared with viewers of Black Entertainment Television (BET) and readers of *Jet* magazine as well as her interviews/surveys with more than one hundred women seeking relationships and on-air advice. Combined with wit and humor, Patterson empowers single Christian women to learn to love themselves even when they feel unlovable because they are single.

JESUS AND THOSE BODACIOUS WOMEN
Life Lessons from One Sister to Another—Tenth Anniversary Edition
LINDA H. HOLLIES
978-0-8298-1776-8/paper/320 pp/$14.00
Jesus and Those Bodacious Women is well known for its new spins on the stories of biblical women such as Mary Magdalene, the Bent-over Woman, Queen Esther, and Mary, among others. The tenth anniversary edition of this Pilgrim favorite contains spins on the stories of five additional biblical women: Vashti, Jezebel, Cozbi (the prostitute in the book of Numbers), Dorcas, and Lydia. The book is written with the empathy, inspiration, humor, and poignancy characteristic of Hollies. Each chapter includes "Just Between Us" questions and suggestions that will resonate with readers.

SAGE SISTERS
Essential Lessons for African American Women in Ministry
LINDA H. HOLLIES, EDITOR
978-0-8298-1764-5/paper/160 pp/$17.00
Hollies, an experienced minister, put together a collection of essays that gives African American women in ministry and those called to ministry essential learnings needed for success in this male-dominated profession. The options offered and ideas shared all come from sage African American women who have been trailblazers in their various denominations. The denominations included are: African Methodist Episcopal Zion, Baptist, Church of God, United Church of Christ, and United Methodist.

To order these or any other books from The Pilgrim Press call or write to:

THE PILGRIM PRESS
700 PROSPECT AVENUE EAST
CLEVELAND, OHIO 44115-1100

PHONE ORDERS: 1-800-537-3394 ▪ FAX ORDERS: 216-736-2206

Please include shipping charges of $6.00 for the first book and $1.00 for each additional book.

Or order from our web sites at www.pilgrimpress.com and www.ucpress.com.

Prices subject to change without notice.